THE RISE
OF THE
CANADIAN
NEWSPAPER

Perspectives on Canadian Culture

JUDITH SALTMAN
Modern Canadian Children's Books

EUGENE BENSON & L.W. CONOLLY
English Canadian Theatre

DAVID CLANDFIELD
Canadian Film

MICHELLE GADPAILLE
The Canadian Short Story

EDITH FOWKE
Canadian Folklore

DOUGLAS FETHERLING
The Rise of the Canadian Newspaper

THE RISE OF THE CANADIAN NEWSPAPER

Douglas Fetherling

Toronto OXFORD UNIVERSITY PRESS 1990

Oxford University Press, 70 Wynford Drive, Don Mills, Ontario M3C 1J9

Toronto Oxford New York Delhi Bombay Calcutta Madras Karachi
Petaling Jaya Singapore Hong Kong Tokyo Nairobi Dar es Salaam
Cape Town Melbourne Auckland

and associated companies in
Berlin Ibadan

Canadian Cataloguing in Publication Data

Fetherling, Douglas, 1949-
The rise of the Canadian newspaper
(Perspectives on Canadian culture)
Includes bibliographical references.
ISBN 0-19-540707-5

1. Canadian newspapers - History. I. Title.
II. Series.

PN4904.F47 1990 071'.1'09 C90-093724-6

1 2 3 4 - 3 2 1 0
Printed in Canada

FOR NEIL REYNOLDS

CONTENTS

PREFACE

The inherent danger in a brief survey of the evolution of the newspaper press is that one will accumulate a great many unrelated facts but lose the historical thread. One risks ending up with a lot of data but no ideas, thereby trivializing the institution about which one is writing. Yet a few previous commentators on the subject have avoided this pitfall, allowing the patterns of development to arise naturally from their narrative. I have attempted to do the same here, within the length limitations of the Perspectives on Canadian Culture series.

In trying to metabolize much of the recent research in this field, both the scholarly and the vernacular, I have been forced to conclude that the story of the press has not been necessarily the way that television has usurped so much of its power, though that is certainly one part of the drama. It seems to me that the heart of the matter, rather, is the way that the press, born as a tool of government, gradually became an instrument of various political parties instead, and freed itself of that role only to undergo, long before television or even commercial radio, an extraordinary period of restructuring.

Politics, demographics, technology, and other factors came together to ensure that in each city where formerly there had been a variety of smaller daily newspapers, there now would be only a single very much larger one or at most two. Societal changes, quite apart from the question of rival media, were at the back of this transition, just as corporatism in general, and chain ownership in particular, were often the means though not usually the cause. In any case, the effect was the same: to rob daily newspapers of their most important asset—their localness. That much of their community function was then picked up by others was a crucial occurrence, but a slightly later one perhaps.

I am indebted to Professor Donald Swainson for his helpful suggestions about the manuscript.

1

THE COLONIAL AND REFORM PRESS

A great deal of disagreement is possible about the precise origins of the English-language newspaper, but virtually none exists about its basic pattern of evolution. Within a hundred years of the invention of movable type in the fifteen century, it was apparent that the new medium was useful for transmitting information about issues of the day, not simply for perpetuating dogma. The discovery of such unrealized potential frightened the powers that be, who commenced a centuries-long period of harassment and intimidation in order to check what today is called the power of the press. Compared to Europe or even what became the United States, newspapering came to Canada rather late in the day, in the second half of the eighteenth century. But once here it took root at once and spread rapidly, and was at all times informed by the long tradition of persecution and bravery, woe and triumph.

The early printers made way for newspapers as we know them now through a process of trial and error, but by the latter half of the seventeenth century the end result was clear. It was at this time, in England and western Europe, that several types of specialty publication arose in the field of current events and business that were indebted to the newsletters of the Renaissance. An *advertiser* was just that, a sheet for merchants with bits of non-commercial news thrown in, while a *mercury* was more on the order of an almanac or olio of information in a form less permanent than a book; a *gazette* was concerned mostly with public affairs. Then there were distinctions reflecting frequency as much as content. A *journal* was a publication that recounted recent events in serial or instalment form, and a *diurnal* arranged the material in chronological order under the day on which the events took place. Most such publications appeared no oftener than once a week. They employed essentially the same technology found in Gutenberg's day, which was much refined but little changed for 300 years: a frame (wooden, but later of iron) on which the type was placed, inked, and covered by paper, the impression resulting when a screw brought pressure on the sheet to be imprinted. It seems crude, but its political ramifications, and its potential for casting public opinion, were obvious to the authorities from the first.

The repressive measures proceeded apace with the spread of the craft. Elizabethan and Stuart printers, for instance, were kept on a short leash indeed lest they undermine the Crown. A decree of 1637 went so far as to strike at the roots by limiting the number of English type foundries to only four. By 1665, the founding year of the *Oxford Gazette*—the 'paper of news' that is generally acknowledged as the first English newspaper in the modern sense—printers were leading precarious lives indeed if they exercised their latent power and began to help shape opinion. In fact it was because of persecution that newspapering crossed the Atlantic to the American colonies and thence moved northward to present-day Canada. In 1690 a printer named Benjamin Harris quit an English gaol where he had spent two years in lieu of paying fines, and immigrated to Boston, where he began the first North American newspaper. It was called *Publick Occurrences Both Foreign and Domestick*, and its name is a pretty accurate summary of what it, and its many later imitators, contained. Others to follow in Boston were the *Boston News-Letter* (1704) and the *New England Courant* (1721). The former was published by John Campbell who, like many colonial printers, was also a local postmaster and was thus able to send his publications to subscribers without charge, though most newspapers were printed in editions of only a few hundred copies, which were usually passed on by hand. The *New England Courant* was founded by James Franklin, whose brother Benjamin Franklin would later play an important role in the Canadian as well as the American press.

The New World did not necessarily offer the freedom the printers had wished for. In fact, being a colonial society it was, in some ways, more harsh on those who dared to criticize its working, for there were two levels of authority to be feared: the government in London and its local emissaries and appointees. In 1735 a German immigrant named John Peter Zenger was charged with criminal libel for criticizing the colonial governor in his *New-York Weekly Journal,* but the case was dismissed by a grand jury. The decision is still hailed as a landmark in the fight for press freedom, but the victory was to some extent a pyrrhic one since, by that time, a far more serious grievance had assumed shape.

The source of contention was the Stamp Act, first enacted in 1712, by which London taxed each printed piece of paper in Britain as a means of increasing prices and thus prohibiting circulation among the poorer, less-educated classes who might have their dissatisfactions fanned. A generation later, when the tax was extended to the North American colonies as a means of levying support for the military presence there, it quickly became a focal-point for disobedience and, eventually, for the armed revolt from which Canadian publishing was to profit.

No newspapers were published in Canada until the time of the Conquest. In fact it was long held by historians that not a single printing press existed in New France during the whole of the *ancien régime*; but it is now known that one such piece of equipment was indeed brought over but was used, apparently, only for religious printing. It remains an unassailable irony, however, that printing became a part of Canadian society only with the establishment of British rule and, moreover, that nearly all the earliest printers were Americans.

Printing was a skilled trade in an age when trades were nurtured and valued. Such knowledge was often passed from father to son and, surprisingly often for the period, from father to daughter or from husband to widow as well. Bartholomew Green (1699-1751), Canada's first newspaperman, was the son of the man who printed the *Boston News-Letter*. After apprenticing with his father, he began publishing his own paper, the *Boston Gazette*.

His motives in removing to Canada were clear enough: he was commissioned as a lieutenant of artillery and sent to Louisbourg on Cape Breton Island, from which place he returned briefly to Massachusetts before settling finally in Halifax and opening a printing office in Grafton Street in 1751. Green issued a prospectus for a Halifax newspaper operation but died before the plans could be realized, whereupon one of his old Boston partners, John Bushell (1715-61), landed at the town and revived or appropriated the idea. The first issue of Bushell's *Halifax Gazette* appeared in March 1752. It was from this paper that not only today's Halifax *Chronicle-Herald* but all of Canada's daily journalism might be said to derive. Even were this not the case, it would be well to remember Bushell and his paper, for both seem fairly typical of the period that immediately commenced. In 1776 Canada got its first female printer when Margaret Draper (1704-1807?) fled Boston for Halifax with her business partner John Howe. She stayed only a few months before removing to England.

Like Green, Bushell was a good craftsman and seems to have taken pride in the legibility of his typography. Like most colonial printers, he had to be a generalist in order to support himself. For instance, it is likely that he did job-printing for Halifax merchants. The biggest patron of docile printers, however, was the same government that in the mother country had always been the scourge of uppity ones: much of Bushell's income came from commissions to produce copies of new laws and proclamations. Such legal matter was also a main ingredient in his newspaper, the rest consisting of political articles scalped from British and sometimes European publications months after they had first appeared, as well as much localized information relating to the town's position as a trade centre: shipping news and reports on developments in the American and Caribbean colonies.

The *Gazette* was printed two columns wide on both sides of a sheet of foolscap (even seventy-five years later most colonial papers were quarto or even octavo and seldom more than four pages) and carried merchants' announcements of newly arrived goods for sale (the forerunner of display advertising), as well as notices of misplaced spouses, delinquent indentured servants, and runaway slaves (the period's equivalent of classified advertising). Like most contemporary printers, who often inserted their own advertisements offering to purchase rags, Bushell must have found paper in short supply at times, though Halifax, being so active a port, no doubt gave him an advantage in that regard. The *Quebec Gazette* sometimes had to suspend publication for want of paper.

Again, as with so many other printers, Bushell frequently ran afoul of the law, though in his case the trouble came from indebtedness more than outspokenness. He lost control of the paper within a few years, though his bankruptcy might also be related to the rumour, never proved in surviving accounts, that he was a notable drunkard as well. The *Gazette* struggled on, but not until 1766 was there another Halifax newspaper. And not until 1769, with the brief appearance of the *Nova Scotia Chronicle and Weekly Advertiser*, did what is now modern Canada have a newspaper totally free of patronage from the oligarchy. When the publication collapsed, its proprietor, a German named Anthony Henry (1730?-1801), returned to his old post as King's Printer. By that time the press in British North America was already facing its first serious test in the political ferment that culminated in the revolt of the thirteen southern colonies, a contest from which it would emerge triumphant.

It has been irresistibly tempting for American historians to exaggerate the importance of the contentious Stamp Act in the events leading to the Revolution—often to the disadvantage of the Quebec Act, for example. The Stamp Act affected newspapers directly, thus giving them reason to use to the fullest their new power to influence discussion. There is some significance, for example, in the fact that after 1769, one of the years when protest was strongest, presses began to be manufactured in New York. One would do well to consider the ramifications of the Act on Canadian printing, particularly the way it provoked an influx of Loyalist printers, and also the way it caused the American rebels to attempt to sway Canada to their cause, thus clearing the ground for both newspaper competition and the Canadian party press. In 1757 the British government had increased the tax in England,

and in 1776, needing to finance certain military requirements in America, boosted it there as well—but by this time the war had broken out. The tax was not reduced in Britain until 1836 and survives today in the form of postage stamps required on certain legal documents, such as wills and leases. It was as unpopular in some Canadian circles as in American ones, and some Canadian newspaper proprietors either ceased publication or faced punishment as a result of its strictures. On the day in 1776 when the reinforced act came into effect, for instance, the *Quebec Gazette*, which called itself '*la plus innocente Gazette de la domination britannique*', simply suspended publication with a whimper rather than pay up, even though it opened its columns to more opposition once it resumed later. That same year the *Halifax Gazette* was banned outright for similar reasons. But though there were some sympathizers for the American cause, they were found mainly in Montreal among former residents of the southern colonies or those whose livelihood depended on trade with the more populous areas to the south. The Act, and its various successors, may have been unpopular in Canada, but they were not the symbol for other grievances, as was the case in the future United States. The fact that the colonies to the north remained loyal, however, was not for want of trying to sway them on the part of the American printers.

In 1775, at the opening of the rebellion, there were 37 newspapers in the American colonies, as compared with 50 in London itself; they included a few loyalist journals such as that published by James Rivington in New York, *Rivington's New York Gazetteer; or the Connecticut, Hudson's River, New-Jersey, and Quebec Weekly Advertiser*, bearing the masthead 'printed at his Open and Uninfluenced press, fronting Hanover Square'. 'Open and uninfluenced', in this case, referred to independence from prevailing republican thought, and the inclusion of Quebec in the scope of its attention indicates where its sympathies lay and where it hoped its message would fall on friendly ears. The hope was misplaced. Such contact as existed between the Canadian and American colonies during the war was mainly personal, not political, at least until the Americans' capture of Montreal in

November 1775, and their ill-fated siege of Quebec in December. The exceptions were mainly of American origin. The most important was the attempt of Benjamin Franklin to establish, at one remove, a rebel newspaper in Montreal.

Franklin was a printer first and only subsequently a rebel statesman, scientist, inventor, and folk philosopher, and he maintained his involvement in the trade almost until the end of his life, proudly stating that he had always been 'a leather-apron man'. (Nor was he any stranger to Canada, having established the forerunner of the Canadian postal system.) While in London on one of his diplomatic missions, he met a printer named Fleury Mesplet (1734-94), a native of Lyons who had come to England fleeing the royalists and who, subsequent to meeting Franklin, immigrated to Philadelphia. That was in 1773. When, two years later, Montreal fell to the American rebels and the British defenders of Canada withdrew to Quebec, Franklin saw an opportunity to establish a journalistic voice in the newly occupied town, which supported a tiny but influential minority of American merchants and sympathizers. One historian of the Canadian press, Wilfrid Eggleston, has quarrelled with the standard interpretation that Mesplet became Franklin's disciple and general servant on the other side of the St Lawrence at that time. Yet the facts seem clear enough. The rebel Congress approached Mesplet with a commission to go to Montreal and establish there a newspaper that would speak to Canadians, especially French Canadians, of the American cause. Franklin was on a committee that determined the validity of Mesplet's qualifications for the mission; with a few others he even preceded Mesplet to the captured city, as to though to pave the way.

Mesplet departed Philadelphia in March 1776 with his capital converted to Continental currency, the medium of exchange during the American occupation. Shortly after he arrived in Montreal, however, the Americans were forced to evacuate the town, and before he could begin his work Mesplet was imprisoned by the British, who kept him in custody for 26 months. Not until 1778, with the war to the south still raging but with the sovereignty of British Canada restored, was he able to bring out the first issue of a four-page quarto. His original design apparently had been to produce a bilingual paper but, in the early days at least, it was published entirely in French. He called it *La Gazette du commerce et littéraire, pour la ville & district de Montréal.*

La Gazette would be of signal importance today if it had done nothing more than to advance several trends then becoming obvious within the craft, but in fact the publication was more than a useful specimen, for imprisonment had not taken the fire out of Mesplet. His shop was a busy one. In addition to *La Gazette,* he printed a bewildering array of business forms, 'almanacks', and books for use by soldiers, students, priests, and lawyers, as well as a primer of the Iroquois language that is an exquisite rarity today. Such busy-ness may be what prompted Mesplet to hire someone to act as editor of the newspaper itself. Until this time, and in smaller centres for years afterward, editing and printing were not separate functions, just as publishing and bookselling were not separate functions; what we would call letters-to-the-editor were then headed 'letters to the printer' in colonial newspapers. The person Mesplet took on for the distinct role of editor was Valentin Jautard (1738-87), a lawyer who had welcomed the invading rebels in 1775 by declaring that 'our chains are broken, blissful liberty restores us to ourselves . . .'

Both men courted danger. One bout of Jautard's political satire landed the pair of them in gaol; but as the rebellion drew to a close, Mesplet was apparently permitted to escape. He resumed publication yet again, in 1785, but showed no desire to court trouble: the end of hostilities between Britain and what had become the United States made his noisemaking redundant. For years he petitioned the Congress for money he claimed was owed him, but his former patrons no longer favoured him, though he attempted unsuccessfully to enlist the support of John Jacob Astor, who had become America's first great millionaire through shrewd exploitation of the Canadian fur trade.

In 1792 John Graves Simcoe, the newly appointed lieutenant governor of Upper Canada, visited Mesplet's establishment and chanced to meet another printer, Louis Roy (1771-99). A native québécois, Roy had been working in the shop of the *Quebec Gazette/La Gazette de Québec*, and his presence in Montreal at that moment was presumably happenstance. Simcoe offered him the position of first King's Printer in Upper Canada and Roy accepted, travelling to Newark (now Niagara-on-the-Lake) and later, when the capital was moved, to York (Toronto). In addition to the usual proclamations and other official printing expected of the occupant of the post, Roy published the *Upper Canada Gazette; or American Oracle* under government patronage; Mrs Simcoe noted in her famous diary that Roy 'cannot write good English'.

Roy was well paid but dissatisfied; in 1794 he returned to Lower Canada, leaving the paper to continue under other appointees. In Montreal he purchased equipment and began another newspaper called both the *Montreal Gazette* and *La Gazette de Montréal*, and now began what was Canada's first newspaper rivalry. By then Mesplet was dead, and his executors had sold his equipment to one Edward Edwards, who began his own publication, which he also called *La Gazette de Montréal*. Thus the town had two publications competing fiercely for survival in spite of not distinguishing themselves one from the other by name. This situation continued for two years. In the end Edwards triumphed, partly because he was also Montreal's postmaster and could retard delivery of foreign news to his rival. Despite the fact that he held Simcoe's sanction, there is some evidence that Roy too was at least a secret republican. He eventually decamped for New York, leaving the field clear for Edwards—though later another printer, William Brown (1726-89), recomplicated matters by launching yet another Montreal paper and calling it the *Canadian Gazette*. Roy died in his voluntary exile. Edwards went bankrupt in 1808 and sold his assets to Brown, who had changed the name *La Gazette de Montréal* to the *Montreal Gazette*. Much later, in 1822, Brown himself sold out to another Scot, Thomas Andrew Turner, a wealthy merchant, for by then the era of the printer-publisher was receding, at least in such a major centre as Montreal had become. It is Brown's Montreal *Gazette* that continues to be published under that name—of that there is no question. One might also stretch a point, as the present proprietors of the *Gazette* enjoy to do, and say that today's newspaper is the offspring of

Mesplet's attempt at a bilingual republican mouthpiece, though the line of descent would seem to be at best only collateral, not lineal.

For every disturber of the peace in Mesplet's time, there had been several Loyalist printers to counter such revolutionary urges, and it is from them that much of the press in eastern Canada derives. In New Brunswick, for instance, newspapers were introduced in 1783 by several different proprietors, some of whom had worked for the British occupation forces in New York and, following the peace settlement, found it expedient to relocate in Saint John. The first to arrive was John Ryan, a native of Rhode Island. New Brunswick was part of Nova Scotia until the next year, and so Ryan's paper was first named the *Royal St John's [sic] Gazette and Nova Scotia Intelligencer*; it later underwent several name changes, ending as the *Saint John Gazette*. Ryan and his partner were brought up for libel several times after taking to task the government and even the municipal authorities. When his partners returned to the States, Ryan passed control of the paper to a relative in order to accept the position of King's Printer. In time he went to Newfoundland as King's Printer there, and established that colony's first newspaper, the *Royal Gazette and Newfoundland Advertiser*, which he published until his death in 1847. The pattern was similar in Prince Edward Island. The *Royal American Gazette*, begun at Charlottetown in 1787 by the King's Printer, James Robertson (1740-1810?), a Scot by birth but by now a former American, was almost identical to papers he had previously published at New York and later at Shelburne in Nova Scotia. In Upper Canada, Gideon Tiffany (1774-1854), another American, succeeded Louis Roy as King's Printer; in addition to his official duties, he worked with his brother to start two newspapers at Niagara.

There were other printers as well. They all may not have ascended to the lucrative government printing contracts that might have kept them both fed and in their place, but they tended towards similar sentiments in their allegiance to the Crown and in their hasty departure from areas where such devotion was now, suddenly, unfashionable and perhaps even lethal. Looked at in lengthy retrospect and with an eye for continuity, one sees them as individuals whose lives were tumultuous and peaceful by turns. In that respect they anticipated the next generation of Canadian journalists, the Tories and Reformers who fought the long battle over responsible government.

One of the little-remembered turning-points in that particular struggle took place on an evening in July 1832 at a country house in Kensington, then one of the suburbs of London. William Lyon Mackenzie (1795-1861), the radical Scots publicist, indefatigable founder of newspapers, and soon to be the first mayor of Toronto, dined with William Cobbett, the great English journalist, reformer, and troublemaker. Cobbett, who was his senior by nearly three decades, had long been one of Mackenzie's heroes and models. For more than a dozen years Mackenzie had been editing various political newspapers in Upper Canada, stirring up in himself and others the populist wrath that would culminate later in rebellion. At the time of this meeting, in fact, he had already been expelled from the House of Assembly on several occasions, been burnt in effigy once (not for the last time), and been twice the victim of mobs who wrecked his printing shop. One wishes for a transcript of their conversation, but all we have is a letter by Mackenzie to a friend back in Canada, describing Cobbett as 'evidently a man of an ardent temperament, of strong and powerful passions, and I believe his object is to increase the comforts and lessen the misery of the great body of people; but it is evident he is not very scrupulous as to the means of bringing about this great good.' This wonderful assessment of Cobbett was equally appropriate to Mackenzie himself.

In the generation after the Loyalist migrations, the newspapers of British North America began growing in numbers, if not in scope. By the end of the War of 1812 there were twenty papers in all, with an aggregate circulation of about 2,000 copies; of these, five were published in Lower Canada and only one in the upper province. Despite having risen to the level of propaganda during the war, they were still pretty much what newspapers had been during the Enlightenment: journals of ecumenical rationalism, full of scientific and literary materials picked up from foreign publications and used to fill the columns between the official proclamations and what in some cases amounted to plentiful advertising, much of it related to land sales, shipping schedules, and the like. Canadian towns were still small enough to pass most local news by word of mouth, even though a place like Montreal had progressed to the point of having two stable competing newspapers after the *Herald* was established in 1811. As for foreign news, it was usually copied from British and American papers long after the fact. In June 1801, for instance, the *Upper Canada Gazette* at York republished an account of Nelson's victory at Copenhagen in April; and this was not atypical. The thirst for faraway news was simply greater than the capacity to transfer it to local publications, and so many citizens of York, for example, relied on New York and even Boston newspapers to fill the gap.

The situation would change only after the number and variety of newspapers increased, along with the population. By 1824 there were seven newspapers in Upper Canada and a dozen in Lower Canada. By 1833 a metal printing press was being manufactured at York. By 1836 there were fifty newspapers in both the Canadas, and the balance had tipped in favour of Upper Canada, which was home to sixty per cent of them. Of course by this time the changing nature of politics had caused the newspapers to break along party lines, for the struggle between Tories and Reformers that preceded responsible government was about to erupt into open if rather pathetic conflict. It is here that Cobbett's indirect influence was at its height.

Cobbett is remembered partly as the person who finally established the public's right of access to parliamentary debates. John Milton had taken part in the struggles about the privileged nature of parliamentary discourse in England. So had Defoe in his day, and Dickens in his. Cobbett, however, is the figure who established lasting precedence, setting up a business to publish the parliamentary debates that he later, during one of his frequent financial embarrassments, sold to a family named Hansard, who lent their own name to the enterprise. In Upper Canada the pioneer was an Irish youth, Francis Collins (1801?-34), whose *York*

Weekly Post began in 1821 to report the words spoken in the Assembly. In time Egerton Ryerson entered the fray with his *Christian Guardian*, the predecessor of the *United Church Observer*. In Lower Canada, *La Minerve* and *Le Canadien* bravely pursued the same ends, while in the Atlantic colonies it was Joseph Howe in the *Novascotian* who deserves, and receives, most of the glory for reporting parliamentary discourse. The sessions at Fredericton were also reported in a local paper, and in 1831 a group of Saint John citizens took up a subscription to pay the salary of a short-hand reporter to travel to the capital on behalf of themselves and other readers.

But Cobbett is also important because of his general fieriness, which remained the same through his Tory intervals as through his periods as a Whig. His life was closely bound up with Chartism and with such events as the passage of the first Reform Act in 1832. Yet, like only a few earlier intellectuals such as Franklin and Thomas Paine, Cobbett was a transatlantic public figure, and his heyday also coincided with the administration of President Andrew Jackson, the backwoods populist who hated banks and the paper currency upon which they profited. In fact, Cobbett published a two-volume life of Jackson, which Mackenzie advertised in his paper for sale in his Toronto shop.

Scholars have long debated the influences on Mackenzie's behaviour and thought. There is, for instance, the ongoing controversy about the extent to which his motives were linked ideologically to those of Jackson and his hooligans across the border. Certainly there is no question but that he took sustenance from English populists as well, particularly Joseph Economy Hulme. But in his role as a journalist, which is what concerns us here, he was clearly under the spell of Cobbett, whom he frequently quoted in his newspaper. They were both inveterate founders of newspapers on the slightest provocation, and both were writers of brisk and intimidating ability, and on occasion prolixity as well—busybodies of unkillable curiosity and widely cast opinions and prejudices. Cobbett, for instance, came to hate the Tories and the Whigs alike, not to mention paper money and Italian opera (in this last, anticipating Ruskin). Both men struggled against class origins they thought were keeping them down: Cobbett as a simple country lad from Farnham, Mackenzie as a Scot who saw other Scots, such as John Strachan, who became the Church of England Bishop of Toronto in 1839, acquiring prestige and power that were denied him.

There is little evidence that the Mackenzie who arrived in Upper Canada in 1820 had any intention of becoming a journalist, for he had not been apprenticed in the printer's craft in Scotland. For the first few years he made his living, first at York and later at Dundas, as a merchant. He was a partner in a drug and book business, though advertisements make clear that the shops were in fact more like general stores and that the literary portion was perhaps little more than a lending library. Of course Mackenzie had the latent talent to be a journalist, as well as the interest, and he was always of a political mind; what's more, he was a great devourer of two- and three-decker novels when such books were read almost exclusively by women. In any case he sold his interest in the business and moved to Queenston, thinking to set up as a bookseller—that is, as a book dealer and publisher—with perhaps an occasional political broadsheet produced on the side. Thus the first issue of the famous *Colonial Advocate* appeared at Queenston in 1824. But within months, increasingly drawn by political intrigue, he moved to the capital, York.

It is not necessary here to restate the political conditions of the time, with social and public life dominated by a tightly knit group of office-holders and merchants who monopolized government patronage and ruled the remote imperial roost with the support of Bishop Strachan. But it is perhaps a good idea to consider the fact that it was of necessity a generation of founders who, being educated and having settled and made the town prosperous, had no recourse but to build up legal and financial infrastructures for it as well. Seen in this light, Bishop Strachan's founding of King's College, the precursor of the University of Toronto, derived from the same instinct as Mackenzie's founding of a newspaper, even though the two institutions were no less poles apart than the two men were. In this connection, too, it is worthwhile to survey the newspaper situation in Upper Canada as it was during and immediately after Mackenzie's arrival.

Inevitably the major force in printing was the King's Printer. Following Louis Roy's return to Lower Canada, the appointment passed to various other persons—one of whom expanded his activities to include an *Upper Canada Almanac*, another of whom, in 1818, increased the appeal of the official organ, the *Upper Canada Gazette*, by abstracting the parliamentary debates of Lower Canada, London, and the United States. Shortly afterward, what must have been subversive elements began creeping into the printing fraternity. With the *Colonial Advocate*, rhetoric became a weapon and Mackenzie himself came to seem, in the eyes of the 'Family Compact' (an epithet coined by Thomas Dalton, editor of the Kingston *Patriot*), the most dangerous man in Upper Canada.

The authorities should have been properly alarmed, for instance, when Charles Fothergill (1782-1840), one of the line of King's Printers, took over the *Upper Canada Gazette* and changed its name to the *Weekly Register*, leaving open the suggestion of homage to Cobbett's renowned *Political Register*. However, the paper continued to refrain from comment in printing the debates from transcriptions made by young Francis Collins. It was in this atmosphere of brewing discontent that Mackenzie and his *Colonial Advocate* arrived in York in 1825 to stir up matters. It seems likely that his presence aroused the others to bolder action. In time Fothergill was sacked, only to begin an independent paper called the *Palladium of British America*, while Collins set up one called the *Canadian Freeman*. By this time there were several other newspapers scattered across Upper Canada that were likewise free of any direct government connection, though all of them relied to a greater or lesser extent on government patronage, which was one of Mackenzie's first causes once he had established himself in a little frame storefront in Duke, now Adelaide, Street.

For all its contemporary and subsequent fame, the *Colonial Advocate* was a queer little newspaper, not at all the last word in its field. In the early days especially (it first appeared as an octavo but soon went broadsheet), its typography was wretched. Mackenzie was no match for Collins, who turned out a clear and well-leaded product and who, incidentally, is said to have been capable of handsetting type for his leaders as he wrote them in his head. By contrast, Mackenzie's five columns of agate must have strained even the voracious eyes of the typical early Canadian who, in Susanna Moodie's words, 'cannot get on without his newspaper any more than an American could without his tobacco'. Its appeal, rather, lay in its bile, which came in several strengths and dosages. Like Cobbett and other autodidacts, Mackenzie was an instant expert on every subject to which he turned his restless mind, be it the latest thoughts of Jeremy Bentham (the great patron of Aaron Burr, who was himself a protégé of Andrew Jackson, whom Cobbett and Mackenzie themselves revered), or the typical Jacksonian idea of the essential perniciousness of banks and paper money. Mackenzie's ultimate crusade was for a vague form of representative government, though the idea evolved slowly before his own and his readers' eyes. It is interesting, however, to scan a volume or two of the *Advocate* to recapture the thousand tiny steps that led to this idea from what at first was simply a generalized hatred of the aristocrats who, in Mackenzie's view, ran the colony as their private park.

May 11, 1826: a caustic 'review' of a sermon by Dr Strachan.

August 3, 1827: a diatribe against banks in general and, in particular, his *bête noire*, the Bank of Upper Canada.

August 16, 1827: a documented attack on government extravagance.

November 29, 1827: a letter, purporting to be from Patrick Swift, a descendant of Jonathan Swift, one of Mackenzie's many *noms de guerre*, warning against the usurpation of power by the scions of the proprietary families.

January 8, 1828: an exposé of how the official class was using and misusing the parliament building itself.

July 9, 1831: a rebuttal of the élitist views on education held tenaciously by Strachan and others.

November 3, 1831: a more generalized lambasting of the Family Compact, the collective term he was now using for everyone he disliked.

And so on. He kept up the offensive, missing no opportunity, no matter how slight the wedge, to attack his enemies.

When Mackenzie first brought the paper to York, for instance, he raised a howl over the Kingston *Chronicle's* receiving government advertising while he was not. He was soon paid off with this form of patronage in the apparent hope that the whining would cease, but of course the effect was precisely the opposite. From then on the antagonism grew steadily on both sides. An especially ludicrous incident involves the erection of the first monument at Queenston Heights in honour of Sir Isaac Brock, the martyr and hero of 1813; some scamp included a copy of the *Colonial Advocate* in the time-capsule at the base. Returning to York and learning of this outrage, Bishop Strachan ordered the stone cut open and the offending rag removed.

Then there was the matter of legislative debates. The politicians may long since have agreed to the principle of preserving their utterances, but they still did not necessarily favour free public distribution of the reports. Collins had dutifully been taking down the speeches in the Assembly for several years, and for the past two years had been paid out of the public purse for doing so. Then, when he began his *Canadian Freeman*, the legislature cut off his stipend. They also refused to allow the *Colonial Advocate* to republish them, at least until Mackenzie raised a loud alarm and proceeded to send an amanuensis to cover the session when he was unable to go himself. As journalists have learned ever since, it is difficult to be just a little subversive, and life was quite rough on Mackenzie, especially in terms of finances. After about two years of publishing, he thought seriously of giving up political journalism entirely and of making his newspaper into 'a literary and scientific work' of the benign sort. He might well have done so had not good fortune intervened six weeks later in the familiar mask of tragedy and harassment.

One evening in June 1826, while the proprietor was known to be away in Lewiston, NY (having fled there to avoid arrest for debt), a group of fifteen Tory youths, most of them law students, called at Mackenzie's shop in Frederick Street and in a few minutes reduced it to rubble. The press, a new variety of cast-iron

Washington with lever action, was heavily damaged. Four pages of type set for the next issue were ruined and, along with other type 'dissed' in cases, were spewed over the floor, the yard, and the garden of a neighbouring house; and the compositors' stone (in those days actually a slab of stone) was broken. Some of the type (but not the press, as is commonly supposed) was thrown into the bay that lapped the shore directly across the street. That done, the youths, who were under at least the tacit leadership of Sheriff Samuel Peter Jarvis, a frequent victim of Mackenzie's pen, dispersed.

It seems that the mob had not formed in response to a particular political barb. A century later Hector Charlesworth gave voice to the accumulated gossip by suggesting that Mackenzie 'had assaulted the moral character of the wives and daughters of members of the alleged Family Compact.' As attacks on newspaper offices went, it was a rather well-planned and orderly affair; certainly it doesn't stand up to the record of violence implied by the name given it in history: the Type Riot. But all the same it was an absolutely crucial event for Mackenzie, swinging still more public support his way because it destroyed the Compact's reputation for civility and peace. He quickly bought some second-hand type 'on the frontier' with the US and was back in operation. Refusing an offer from Jarvis to settle out of court for £300, he pressed claims for damages and eventually was awarded the magnificent sum of £625. With that money Mackenzie refitted the shop in a way he could never have afforded before, so that the paper's circulation could increase. Also increased was his popularity, which caused him to stand for and win a legislative seat himself. This was in 1828, one of the pivotal years in the development of the press in the region.

While all this was taking place, Francis Collins in his own publication made the mistake of attacking his powerful enemies once too often and too violently. For a particular reference to the attorney general's 'native malignancy', he was sent to gaol, where he continued to turn out copy from his cell. But in a countervailing victory, Mackenzie manoeuvred successfully to have himself awarded the contract for printing the legislative debates, a fact that irritated those printers who supported the *status quo*, such as Robert Stanton, who had changed the name of the *Upper Canada Gazette* to the *United Empire Loyalist*, and his predecessor, a former army surgeon, now a teller at the Bank of Upper Canada—whose house Mackenzie took satisfaction in personally setting alight in the 1837 uprising. It was becoming clear that Mackenzie was more than simply the village scold, eager to enjoin the established order to better behaviour, like some opposition leader with no hope of ever gaining a majority of his own. Rather he was beginning to use the Compact's own weaknesses to wrest power from them, peacefully at first, in order to set up a rival hierarchy that would then change the very nature of government.

In 1829, fuelled by a desire actually to set in motion the kind of democracy he envisioned, Mackenzie went to the United States, visiting New York, Philadelphia, and particularly Washington City, where he was entertained at the White House by President Jackson. He was rapturous. Even Mackenzie's first and most adulatory biographer, his son-in-law Charles Lindsey, would allow that Mackenzie had gone to the States 'with a disposition to view everything he saw there in *couleur de rose*.' On his return he utilized his characteristic energy to address what was perhaps also his characteristic shortage of cash and dashed off a book about what he had observed. It bore a dedication to Cobbett.

Rather a good deal is known about Mackenzie's business practices because he tended to provide readers with full accounts of his deals, and it is well to dip into such information, as it tends to make him seem part of the profession overall rather than a single journalistic rabblerouser. For instance, he appeared to perform most editorial functions himself, writing virtually all of whatever paper he was putting out and probably not trusting anyone else to clip from the publications he received on an exchange basis. One contemporary describes Mackenzie 'sitting at his parliamentary desk, in his stocking feet, the busiest man in the House; with paste pot and scissors before him, pouring over the "exchanges" or transferring cuttings from them ready to be commented upon in his paper . . . as soon as he found leisure.' It is known that he had equipment to help bind not only his own tracts but the blank books he sold along with various other stationery items. Some insight into the business is provided by the fact that a scant few weeks before the outbreak of rebellion in 1837, he travelled to a sort of booksellers' convention in New York to buy thousands of books needed to restock his retail shelves. The list of titles, as set out in house-advertisements, is of interest in showing the extent to which he was a respectable enough printer and bookseller, serving the community in a non-controversial way even while he was the centre of tumultuous political intrigues. He had on hand 2,000 copies of the *Westminster Assembly's Shorter Catechism*, 404 copies of *Brown's Bible Concordance*, and smaller quantities of the standard texts in chemistry, geology, education, and mathematics including algebra, as well as various literary favourites and, rather ominously in the circumstances, 29 copies of a work called *Dyckman's Manual of Military Exercises*.

In keeping with the practice of the time, Mackenzie took in a number of apprentices. Their duties probably consisted of running errands, sweeping out the place, clerking, cleaning the type of its 'lice' with lye and water, struggling with the paper-stretchers, melting the contents of the hell-box for re-use as leads and slugs, and then—once they had begun to acquire some of the skills they had come to master—composing type in the stick, transferring it to the stone, using type furniture to make a snug fit before moving it from the stone to the chase, which would then go to the press. One of the apprentices was his apparently illegitimate son James, who in time became a newspaper editor in the US. Another was a lad whose surname has come down to us as Falls. In 1830, when another mob, unrelated to the first, attacked the *Advocate* and began breaking up the place, Falls loaded a weapon, presumably a musket, with sticks of type and fired at the intruders, and then had to flee across the border in fear of his life.

Mackenzie continued to immerse himself in the ever-deepening gumbo of partisan struggle. Upon his return from England, where he had gone carrying petitions to the authorities about conditions in Upper Canada, he again considered giving up publishing newspapers, except for a few special issues at irregular intervals.

This time the decision stuck. In November 1834 the last issue of the *Advocate* appeared. Its name and subscription list were then sold to the proprietors of the struggling *Correspondent*, which became the *Correspondent and Advocate*, an early example of a newspaper merger. Mackenzie kept back what are described as a new iron press, a second-hand press of some sort, a large powerful 'standing press', a small job press, and his 'annual' supply (or 'dress') of type. With the proceeds of the sale he circulated various political documents directly to the people at his own expense. But in the summer of 1836 he was at it again, with a new paper called the *Constitution*, a four-page weekly like the *Advocate*, but a huge seven-column 'horse blanket' this time, its front page given over entirely to serious news—a presentation that put it in the vanguard. Its advertisements, which Mackenzie seemed to have had more luck soliciting than in the past, were confined for the most part to the fourth page. He gave much attention to this paper even while he was organizing radicals within the province and liaising with Louis-Joseph Papineau about the prospect of simultaneous armed uprisings in the two Canadas. He was still putting it out almost up to the point when hostilities erupted in December 1837.

In Nova Scotia the journalistic career of Joseph Howe (1804-73) presents a different picture. His brand of reform—pro-British rather than pro-American, and certainly less radical—was conspicuously more successful. His effective and highly dramatic defence against libel in 1836 (he had charged 'that from the pockets of the poor and distressed, at least one thousand pounds are drawn yearly, and pocketed by men whose services the country might very well spare'—the police and magistrates, to be precise) was the greatest single legal victory for the press in early Canada; yet he was not careless with words the way Mackenzie was, nor certainly with deeds either. When, in 1847, Nova Scotia became the first colony to win responsible government, he could claim with some justice that the goal had been achieved without 'a blow struck or a pane of glass broken'. And whereas Mackenzie was a habitual beginner of newspapers, ready to abandon or substantially change them when their immediate political purpose no longer suited him, Howe was acutely conscious of the newspaper's place in developing and sustaining the society that patronized it, a role that rested firmly on a bed of continuity. He was the son of the loyalist John Howe, the postmaster general and King's Printer who had founded the Halifax *Journal* after he and Margaret Draper had been forced to abandon their *Massachusetts Gazette*. The young Howe thus grew up learning the craft and understanding that he could 'always provide for myself by starting a paper either here or elsewhere'. He spent a year publishing a Halifax paper called the *Acadian* before assuming control from George R. Young in December 1827 of the *Novascotian*, which under his direction asserted its importance by leading the struggle for the right to print legislative debates and by championing numerous other causes. Howe believed in the educational role of the press, and the dissemination of knowledge was a frequent byproduct of all the policies argued in the *Novascotian*'s pages. In contrast to Mackenzie, Howe valued printing as a craft in itself. The *Novascotian* was a small paper distinguished by its stately design and the high, even quality of his reproduction, to say nothing of the evidence it provided of Howe's love of the *Spectator* and the *Tatler*, an editorial inclination that paralleled Fleury Mesplet's affection for Voltaire and Diderot.

As Canadian cities assumed shape, their newspapers became more numerous, more transient, more specialized, more openly partisan, in fact—and certainly louder. In this sense, the future favoured the Mackenzies over the Howes.

2

TOWARDS CONFEDERATION

In an 1834 publication called *A New Almanack for the Canadian True Blues*, Mackenzie inventoried the newspapers of British North America, dividing them into camps. The *Novascotian* and 14 others—including the Kingston *Spectator*, the Grenville *Gazette*, and two French-language ones, *Le Canadien* and *La Minerve*—he applauded as 'patriotic liberal journals'. An equal number—including the *Courant* and the *Gazette* of Montreal, and the *Herald and Chronicle* of Kingston—he characterized as 'servile Tory papers'. Two others, one in Montreal and the other in York, had 'not decided yet'.

The list was by no means complete, but it nonetheless tells us a good deal. It reminds us first of all what an extraordinary number of papers were sharing a small audience (in 1824, all but two of the newspapers had circulations of 400 copies or less). It also shows how polarized they were, even within a given community. It shows how partisan concerns cut across language lines in Lower Canada, where anglophone editors such as Dr Jocelyn Waller, Dr E.B. O'Callaghan, and Daniel Tracey were as much a part of Louis-Joseph Papineau's political apparatus as a francophone editor such as Étienne Parent. Also, it at least suggests how the party press and the fierce newspaper competition of years to come had their roots in the fact that many places had both Reform and Tory papers; this was true not just of Toronto or Montreal but of Saint John, for example, where the Reform *Courier* fought the Tory *Herald*, or of Pictou, where it was the *Chronicle* versus the *Observer*. By the same token, Mackenzie's list implies how, in the more important centres, two papers might be combined into one if circumstances warranted. Most usefully of all, it presents a sketch of a journalistic landscape that was just about to change.

In the inevitable period of repression that followed the uprisings of 1837-8, but preceded responsible government, the Tories virtually eliminated the Reform press.

Tory mobs wrecked some Reform papers, such as Donald McLeod's Grenville *Gazette*, and one Mackenzie did not enumerate, S.P. Hart's Belleville *Plain Speaker*. Hart removed himself to Cobourg, a safe distance away, and grew more moderate, or perhaps simply newsier, at the expense of unrelieved opinion, whereas others acted pre-emptively before the rioters could assemble. When such a crowd smashed the Montreal *Vindicator*, however, the proprietor, Edmund O'Callaghan, fled the country. The mob that broke the windows and wrecked the type cases of the *British Whig* in Kingston, and even killed the editor Edward Barker's dog, wore masks. A gang of thugs attacked the editor of the St John's *Ledger* in Newfoundland and cut off his ears; later they gave his press foreman the same treatment. The London *Free Press* was wrecked by a political mob as late as 1849, after responsible government had already come to Upper Canada, or Canada West as it had become. Étienne Parent (1802-74), editor of *Le Canadien*, whose motto was '*Nos Institutions, Nos Langue et Nos Lois*', went to prison briefly in 1838, as did Francis Collins of Toronto, who was sentenced in 1828 to a year for his criminal libel on the attorney general, who called it 'one of the miserable consequences of the abuse of liberty, that a licentious press is permitted to poison the public mind with the most absurd and wicked misrepresentations.' The list of others who were jailed included the editor of the *Niagara Spectator* and a pamphleteer in Nova Scotia, William Wilkie.

Yet responsible government brought with it a new role for journalists, who began their period of greatest influence in society. The beneficiaries were a different generation from the old rebels, however, and their ability to use power rested partly on social and technological factors quite beyond the scope or control of party politics.

George Brown (1818-80) was unquestionably the most important editor of the new sort. In the year of Mackenzie's rebellion, he left Edinburgh for New York in company with his father, and in 1843 they arrived in Toronto to begin a Free Kirk journal called the *Banner*. With sound commercial instincts, the younger Brown noted the almost unnatural absence of any whiggish paper. Upholding strong political convictions, he felt the need for a sheet that would nudge and cheer the responsible-government movement, with which he had quickly taken up. Thus, in 1844, he began a four-page weekly, the *Globe*, which was a reform organ only briefly, until becoming an institution in its own right—at times, almost a party in its own right.

At this point daily newspapers in Canada had not been successful. The first one in British North America, the *Daily Advertiser*, founded in 1833, proved too ambitious for even so important a market as Montreal. It was followed in Toronto, in 1836, two years after Toronto's incorporation as a city, by the even more short-lived *British Standard*. As Canadian communities expanded, they were served instead by weeklies, bi-weeklies, and, most importantly, tri-weeklies, including at least one that boasted of its frequency in its name, the *Tri-Weekly Herald* of London.

As late as December 1860 Howe's *Novascotian* carried an advertisement announcing: 'THE "COLONIAL EMPIRE" A Political and Commercial *Weekly*, *Semi-Weekly*, and *Tri-Weekly Newspaper*, to be published in the City of Saint John, NB, commencing January 1st, 1861.' The prospectus made a vivid distinction between the weekly edition, 'intended to be a first class Commercial Paper [containing] not only the latest Shipping and Market Reports from all parts of our own and sister Provinces, but also what relates to ourselves at British and Foreign Ports', and the semi-weekly, 'made up expressly for Country circulation'. Both in turn were quite separate from the tri-weekly, 'devoted more particularly to City matters and general news'. In cities where two competing tri-weeklies began to publish on alternating days, it became clear that there were enough readers and advertisers to support at least one daily instead. Another intermediate stage was represented by seasonal dailies, such as the *Herald* and the *Gazette* in Montreal, which for some years appeared each day only during the warmer months, when the port was busy.

So Brown's *Globe* moved prudently first to bi-weekly and then to thrice-weekly (Tuesday, Thursday, and Saturday) status, carefully building a constituency for a general newspaper that would marshal valuable information from a variety of sources for the commercial and professional classes. When Brown finally moved to daily publication in 1853, a number of other papers had preceded him, such as the *British Whig* of Kingston, which went to daily status in 1849, and the Saint John *Morning Times*, which followed in 1852, providing reassuring proof of the notion that news could and should be changed every day, a rather remarkable leap in consciousness in an age when the same could not be said of personal linen. Advertisers, with more goods from more sources and a practical need to turn them over quickly, contributed to the acceptance of the idea that news was a perishable commodity capable of being broken off into daily instalments to accommodate the marketplace (just as it would become a twice-daily phenomenon—6 and 11 p.m.—in the age of network television). The telegraph also aided in this revolution in thinking by making news more international and the object of greater competition.

As a result, more and more dailies began appearing in the 1850s, often with the word *Daily* in the name to alert readers to their freshness and to distinguish them from the weekly editions, which were intended for postal delivery to outlying regions. Virtually all the new dailies were morning papers until 1861, when the Saint John *Globe* switched to evening publication to set itself apart. The change indicated the rise of an industrial labour-force that had no time for leisure until the day's work was done; it also played on the advantages of telegraphy, which allowed news to accumulate during the day. Within a generation, evening papers would outnumber morning ones, and more and more publications would add the distinction *Morning*, *Evening*, or *Daily* to their names—a vogue that did not fade until after the Second World War, when, for example, the Vancouver *Daily Province* became the *Province* and the Toronto *Evening Telegram* became the *Telegram*.

The new urban dailies of the early Victorian period were sometimes modelled—rather hopefully, to be sure—on the emerging breed of American papers rather than on British ones. The sources for such inspiration were several. Benjamin Day had started the New York *Sun* in 1833 by eschewing political speeches and other dense matter to concentrate on police news and neighbourhood reporting. Most other dailies cost six cents per copy retail. His cost was one cent: the birth of the so-called penny press. By 1838 the Saint John *News* could claim to be the first successful penny paper in the empire, as the term became common in England as well, though the penny of Britain and Canada was not strictly of equivalent value to the American cent. Other American influences were James Gordon Bennett the Elder, who started the New York *Herald* in 1835, creating the society page and the notion of daily stock-market quotations, while Horace Greeley followed in 1841 with the *Tribune*, whose tone was lofty and moral by comparison. The New York *Times*, originally intended as another penny paper for the masses, reached a circulation of 20,000 within eleven days of its first appearance in 1851. The bigger the audience, the bigger the paper's potential role in politics; the more sophisticated the readership, the more respected the paper. The line between journalism and party politics was often indistinct. George Monro Grant, principal of Queen's University, was referring to Brown specifically when he commented that 'at this time in the history of the world it was almost impossible to be an editor without being a politician also.'

Mackenzie had now ended his American exile. His return to Toronto was condemned in most local newspapers except the *Examiner*, which a mob therefore threatened to destroy—until it saw that the staff inside had armed themselves. Soon Mackenzie was founding newspapers again, ones livelier in appearance than before but ultimately lifeless, for first-hand experience of the republic had robbed him of his ideology. He and Brown make a fascinating comparison as sociological types. In the legislature as well as in print, Mackenzie had been influential as an irritant. As both a politician and an editor, Brown had genuine power in matters of policy and public debate; and so, in what was rather a quite separate way, did his newspaper.

Technology, specifically the technological opportunities open to Brown that were undreamt of by Mackenzie, must certainly be one factor in the difference. Like Mackenzie, Brown found it prudent to buy an interest in a paper mill; but he made such investments more frequently, and more shrewdly, like the Victorian businessman he was, not like a colonial shopkeeper. Also, he kept a weather eye for ways of applying new developments to his own business in particular. As early as 1876, he joined with the proprietor of the *Mail* to charter a special train that would deliver the two papers to Hamilton and London. The venture was so costly that it helped to ruin the *Mail* eventually, but the *Globe* resumed the practice on its own in 1887 and made it work.

There were no great innovations in the setting of type—none at least with widespread implications, until the last quarter of the nineteenth century; but press work, the other mechanical component of newspaper production, underwent a number of revolutionary changes. The first and most profound was the introduction of the steam-driven printing press, which set in motion the transition of printing from a craft to an industry and also solved the problems raised by growing circulation by making bigger, more frequent papers a reality. In 1814, *The Times* of London became the first newspaper to print by steam, the proprietor outwitting Luddites who were awaiting a pretext to smash the equipment. In Canada, William Cunnabell of Halifax had the first steam-press in 1840 and from then on development was rapid. Although it was actually the result of a long process involving different inventors and tinkers, as such things usually are, the next big step is associated with the New York firm of R. Hoe & Co., whose Canadian agent was George Brown. There were several stages and several different manufacturers, but the ultimate result was the Hoe Type-Revolving Machine of 1848, in which the *formes* of type were affixed to a cylinder, which imprinted the paper as quickly as the sheets could be fed in; thus was much wasted motion eliminated. The presses then became bigger and faster. By the 1860s the true rotary press was born when both the *formes* and the platen revolved and the paper was supplied in rolls rather than sheets; later still, steam was supplanted by petrol or electricity. This basic process remained unchanged for generations.

George Day imported one of the first large steam cylinder presses for the Fredericton *Loyalist*; by 1852 there was one in Charlottetown. When Brown created the daily *Globe* in 1853, he purchased a new press from New York; but the steam engine to run it was made in Kingston and the type he used was cast in Toronto. That same year, by contrast, his opposite number in Montreal was merely adapting a manually operated press to steam. Other suppliers of presses included Gordon, Fairhaven, and Cameron. But until the final decades of the nineteenth century, when Goss presses became common in metropolitan newspapers, the market was clearly dominated by Hoe, whose presses soon grew so large that they required purpose-built newspaper buildings, with the heavy presses at ground level, or in a high cellar, and the composing room above, connected to the editorial coop. It would become common for press buildings to be erected with huge plate-glasses windows giving passersby a view of the printing process, adding another dimension to the complicated symbiosis between the public and its daily newspaper. Yet such technology was highly destructive of other relationships.

The dream of many an apprentice was to become a journeyman and then a master and to publish his own newspaper, of which he would be both editor and printer. When steam presses began appearing in the larger cities, that dream was dashed, or at best exiled to rural areas. Trefflé Berthiaume (1848-1915), the acknowledged *sauveur* of *La Presse*, if not its actual *fondateur*, was surely among the last proprietors of a major Canadian newspaper to have begun as a printer's apprentice (at 15 in his case) rather than as a tyro capitalist. For the apprentices were replaced by unskilled youths doing piece-work. An unskilled boy, paid a pittance, could do the work of a journeyman (wage, $10 per week in 1850) in tending the new presses, which without much in the way of human supervision spewed out printed pages needing only to be gathered and collated. These young minders learned no skills and so were expendable, while the journeymen left the press room and concentrated solely on setting type. The term 'apprentice' would still be applied to boys in the press room, but the chain handed down from the medieval guild ideal was broken. What's more, the capital cost of the new technology was as high as its labour costs were low. In the 1840s a two-cylinder steam press might be priced at $3,000. The Hoe company demanded fifty per cent in cash on delivery but would carry the balance for six months and even accept older equipment as trade-ins. Even at that, a publisher was likely to be indebted for the down-payment, if not to a traditional lender then perhaps to a group of politicians, thus ensuring his usefulness to them.

As cities and circulations grew, so did the bulk and appetite of the presses. In the 1850s the plant of a daily newspaper in a city the size of Montreal or Toronto might turn out 20,000 newspapers per hour on an eight-cylinder press (which thus required the services of eight boys, one per cylinder). By the 1860s the capacity increased, colour became possible, and automatic stacking features eliminated some of the boys' jobs. Brown bragged to his readers in 1867 that his new Hoe Lightning press cost '$15,000 IN GOLD'. But the top of the line, a 10-cylinder Hoe press, was $52,500 in United States funds, freight-on-board—an enormous investment that accelerated competition for the profits necessary to absorb such a figure with relative ease.

Looked at now, the decade 1840-50 seems to be the great watershed period in the development of newspapers, when Canada made the first leap towards urbanization and various technological, social, and political factors came together to alter not simply the fact of the newspaper but the very concept of news. Yet at the same time newspapers still preserved many of their earlier traits. Perhaps the main characteristic of journalism in this period just beginning was its extraordinary birth-rate. The colonial stage, in which the thinness of the population and remoteness of civilization made sustaining newspapers a comparatively difficult achievement, was gone, while the monopolistic era, in which larger papers killed off or gobbled up the weaker ones in a kind of journalistic Darwinism, had not begun. As a result, papers of every type and variety began to appear in chaotic profusion, including ethnic ones and, especially, religious ones. In all, about 3,500 different newspapers have been published at one time or another in what is now Ontario, about 3,000 in what is now Quebec. This great proliferation first began to gain momentum in the late 1840s.

Except in smaller centres, editing and printing were done by different hands, but in the 1840s there were still many newspaper editors whose primary profession was medicine, the law, shopkeeping, or, of course, politics. This was partly owing to the relative smallness of the society, a factor that encouraged sequential, even multiple careers. Another consideration was the way that newspapers, being undercapitalized and thus speculative by nature, were one tested means for immigrants recently arrived from Britain to make their way in the New World. Newspaper offices had also long provided employment for literary people, sometimes for political convenience or political necessity. In the period under review, for example, Major John Richardson, the author of the Gothic romance *Wacousta* (1832), edited newspapers at Brockville as well as at Kingston, where Charles Sangster, the poet, worked for both the *British Whig* and the *Daily News*, while William Kirby, the author of *The Golden Dog* (1877), put out the *Niagara Mail* at Niagara-on-the-Lake. Susanna Moodie called the Canadian newspaper at this juncture 'a strange mélange of politics, religion, abuse, and general information', to which list she might easily have added literature, some of it indigenous, most of it, by later standards, dreadful.

The poet James Reaney has suggested that the unrelieved columns and black rules of the early Victorian newspaper imposed a grid on the Canadian imagination in the same manner that the steel rails of the railway imposed a grid on the physical landscape. But the average newspaper hardly represented a triumph of the academy over the vernacular. The typical paper of the period was still likely to be two broadsheets, fed into the press by hand, each page strictly vertical and columnar in its make-up save for the horizontal name-plate, which was usually in a Gothic or Old English face. The name *Gazette* still carried official connotations and so proprietors avoided it, embracing the opposite suggestion in *Free Press* (implying freedom from government interference, not from party manipulation—on the contrary). Almost every other tried-and-true newspaper name was used again and again, but there was a decided preference for stately and dignified titles when simple ones would not suffice, though some proprietors, in aiming for dignity, achieved comedy instead: the *Looking Glass* and the *Canadian Son of Temperance and Literary Gem* were two Toronto papers of the 1850s. At least some newspapers can be dated broadly by the fashion in names. As news itself became more perishable, titles referring to the latest in technology or transport were exploited: the *Packet*s of Bytown (Ottawa) and Orillia were at length succeeded by the nation's various *Telegram*s and *Telegraph*s. And after a certain point in late-Victorian times, *Intelligencer* developed an unspeakably outmoded ring, which it retained for generations before becoming quaint and finally historic.

The notion that the first page should carry the most important news, or indeed any news at all, found favour only slowly, spurred on by the later insistence of the penny press. To a greater or lesser degree, page one was usually devoted to the forerunner of classified advertising, which might involve the repeated use of small engravings, such as one of a steamship to announce each paid insertion about arrivals and departure, or one of a house, perhaps with smoke emitting from its chimney, to set off each ad concerned with residential property. The Montreal *Herald* of the 1850s was typical in that its front page was entirely made up of such matter; in the 1870s *The Times* of Ottawa was the same, but then it was attempting, even down to the design of its name-plate, to resemble as closely as possible *The Times* of London, which continued to cling to this style until its purchase in 1959 by the Canadian press magnate Roy Thomson, the future 1st Baron Thomson of Fleet. Wholesale merchants and retail shopkeepers were the most frequent buyers of space and would generally advertise the arrival of new goods in some detail but in straightforward language, permitting variation in the type styles and sizes to add emphasis where necessary. The ubiquitous ads for patent medicines—pills and potions to address impotency, menstrual pain, or even illness in general, however serious—were usually couched in hyperbole, and these were the forerunners of national display advertising, with the copy no doubt supplied from the United States. In London, Canada West, where as late as the 1860s the local press competed with a town crier as a vehicle for advertising, it was considered a marketing breakthrough when, in 1857, a single dry-goods merchant purchased an entire page of the *Free Press*.

Gradually the last two pages of four came to be the domain of such display-type advertising, with the front page divided between news and small adverts, and page two given over to subjective editorial matter, whether addressed from the editor to the readers or from the readers to him. Hence, the gradual development of the editorial page, from a mere table-of-contents in colonial papers to a sort of annotated listing of recent events, to independent comment by late-Victorian times, when it became the voice of the institution itself, pronouncing the truth and passing judgement in leaders of assorted sizes and different degrees of indignation. The modern editorial page continues to follow immediately after the longest and most important news stories of the day and to occupy a left-hand page, despite the assumption that right-hand ones are more important because the eye is drawn to them first.

The exchange desk remained a crucially important part of newspaper editing. So great was the confidence that editors would copy from one another, giving proper credit but without payment, that one paper would invite another in a distant city to reprint an item of interest to both and be reasonably certain that the suggestion would be acted upon. For example, a story about the death in Halifax of someone with connections to Hamilton might end with the line 'Hamilton papers, please copy'—and they would. This tradition lasted until surprisingly recent times, at least in cases where the giver was a large metropolitan paper and the recipient a much smaller one.

The fact that information was drawn from so many different sources, and travelled into print at such irregular speeds, contributed to the abstracted and miscellaneous nature of the news that was published. Indeed, some papers ran left-over bits in miscellany columns (headed '*extraits divers*' in Quebec). In addition, many continued to publish literary material, according to the disposition of the editor, though high-minded educational pretensions were commoner in French-language papers, with their faint sense of obligation to the *encyclopaediastes*; at Confederation, the *Pionnier de Sherbrooke* (motto: '*La Patrie avant tout*') proclaimed itself a '*Journal Politique, Agricole, Industriel, Commercial, Littéraire, de Science, et d'Annonces*'. Book excerpts, particularly novels run serially, were an expected part of the editorial package in the 1850s, a tradition that lingered until the 1960s in a few publications such as the Toronto *Star Weekly*, a descendant of the weekly editions that the largest papers provided for rural readers. Paid subscribers, who were urged to band together in 'clubs' and receive a discount, were valued as a separate market quite apart from single-copy purchasers on the street. In 1844, postage on newspapers and other literary materials was reduced in the Canadas, though not, some complained, low enough to allow circulations to rise to what proprietors believed were natural levels. The Maritime colonies, by contrast, charged no postage on newspapers sent to paid subscribers. Finally, in 1854, the Canadas adopted such a policy as well, so long as the papers were mailed from the printing house; the measure was in effect until 1879 and contributed inestimably to the general boom in newspapers.

The field became crowded because the audience was voracious and the potential rewards were great; but the mortality rate was certainly high. And a split appeared between the urban and the rural audience. When the first publishers' protective society, the Canadian Press Association, was started in 1859, the twenty-one founding papers ranged from the Toronto *Globe* and the Montreal *Gazette* on the one hand to the Dundas *Banner* and the Milton *Journal* on the other. That was perhaps the last moment at which such a homogeneous mix of rural, small-town, and urban publishers would seem to have had an important common purpose (though the Imperial Press Conference, a publishers' symposium in which Canadians played a disproportionately large role and that retained its importance until after the Second World War, continued to pay lip-service to this ideal).

By the 1860s at the latest, the small craft-oriented newspaper shop had been driven out of the cities and found refuge in other precincts in the guise of the country weekly. As papers like the *Globe* or the Montreal *Herald* upgraded, they contributed to the brisk trade that was developing in second-hand presses and in second-hand type and type furniture. In the 1840s one could buy a hand-press suitable for newspaper production for perhaps $150, and some individual presses had long and illustrious lives. A Washington-type flatbed press manufactured by Hoe in the 1830s was in operation at the *Daily British Whig* of Kingston until 1881, when it was sold to a smaller paper in a smaller population centre, the Whitby *Gazette*, and then to a smaller one still, the Pickering *News*, which was published by Joseph T. Clark (who later became editor of both the *Toronto Daily Star* and *Saturday Night* and was the father of Gregory Clark, the celebrated *Star* reporter of the 1920s) and his brother James. In 1900 the press was sold to another small paper, then to yet another, before finally being donated to the Upper Canada Village historical park in 1964. Such a sequence of ownership was not particularly unusual. The same sort of knockabout existence would later apply to Linotypes as well, once they became obsolete on metropolitan papers in the 1970s.

In most Canadian and American cities the printers' local is the oldest surviving labour union—a reminder of the days before newspapers were split into opposing internal factions, with middle-class editorial and advertising staff on the one hand and working-class crafts and mechanical personnel on the other. The back-shops of newspapers, where new social and political ideas abounded, were schools for autodidacts, and the way that mechanization had driven journeyman printers to work as compositors could only strengthen their desire for collective action. At the time, labour unions as such were illegal in Canada, but the printing trades had special status based partly on prior existence. There was a Toronto printers' guild in 1832, for example;

London's printers banded together in 1855. The organizations had great self-esteem but less power. Most members were in fact paid by the measure. In London, the rate was 25 cents for each 1,000 ems of type they set, or roughly $9 per week. A typesetter might accept a wage of $9 per week, but he would then lose the possibility of being compensated for bursts of speed or feats of endurance, factors that could push up the total to $11 or even $12 per week. By comparison, typesetters in Hamilton were receiving 26 cents per 1,000 ems, those in Toronto 30 cents. So it was that in 1856 the London *Free Press* informed its readers that 'Journeymen Printers of this place have formed a combination for the purpose of compelling employers to pay them high wages'. A strike ensued. The proprietors would not be moved and took the unusual step of advertising for blacklegs (scabs)—female ones at that. The strike was broken by the darkening cloud of recession that crossed the sky in 1857, a year, incidentally, when the *Globe* led all other Canadian newspapers in circulation, followed by the evangelical and violently anti-Catholic Montreal *Witness*; the national average was 5,700 copies for daily and weekly editions combined, with the latter dominating.

Apart from the introduction of the steam-driven rotary press, the biggest development in newspaper publishing in the Victorian period was undoubtedly the telegraph, which suddenly made news from distant places as easy to obtain as local news—easier, in some ways, since other people did the harvesting of it. It had a hand in promoting local news as well, simply by increasing competition for facts and sharpening and intensifying the very idea of news. That is not to say, however, that its effects were uniformly beneficial in terms of the culture. In the days when overseas news arrived under sail, an editor was likely to receive a packet of newspapers and reports all at once, which would provoke him to write a commentary on the events about which he had just learned, an essay of sorts. With the telegraph, facts overshadowed reactions, news overwhelmed thought. And in time, with a slow and death-like certainty, newspaper prose lost its originality and began to emulate the terse telegraphic style.

The invention itself dates to 1844, the work of the American painter Samuel F.B. Morse, who also devised the Morse code necessary to the system. He tried to sell the invention to his government, but failing, established a private company, which soon had a line extending as far north as Montreal. Progress was spotty. A line linking Toronto and Hamilton was ready in December 1846; another joining Toronto and Montreal came in August 1847, allowing George Brown to station a commercial correspondent at the latter terminus. But points on the east coast were not joined to those in Canada East and Canada West until 1850, though Saint John and Halifax were linked to Boston in 1849 and Saint John and Fredericton were connected the following year. As late as 1876, a disastrous coal-mine explosion in Nanaimo, BC, was reported to eastern Canada via San Francisco because there was no telegraph line across Canada until the completion of the Canadian Pacific Railway almost a full decade later.

Halifax seemed to be a special case. For years reporters had been taking pilot boats from Halifax harbour to meet incoming steamers fifty miles offshore, ransacking them for news and dispatching it back to the mainland by carrier pigeon; with telegraphy, the pigeon network became obsolete. Pigeons had also been the favoured instrument of Paul Julius de Reuter, the founder of the Reuter news agency, but he soon embraced telegraphy and had opened a London office by 1851. The last fifty-mile section of wire tying Halifax to New York was paid for by the American financier Jim Fisk as part of his successful plan to go short on Confederate States bonds. The instant the American Civil War ended in 1865, he sent word via this private wire to a confidential agent in Halifax, who boarded the fastest available steamer, which he had had standing by for this purpose. The agent disembarked at London, where the bonds were still trading at eighty cents on the dollar, before news reached England from any other source.

The first American wire service, the Associated Press, began in 1848 as a pooled effort by six New York papers to cover the American invasion of Mexico; but the development of Canadian wire services was impeded for years by the very railways that allowed telegraphy to spread. For the railways came to enjoy a monopoly on such service, which they did not wish to share. News arriving at a station on the Great North Western Telegraph system, an affiliate of the Grand Trunk Railway, was translated from Morse to English and written out in multiple copies on flimsy sheets of paper that were then sent to the various newspaper offices by runner; the flimsies were called *eassons* after the manager of the service, Robert Farmer Easson.

When the first transatlantic cable was completed in 1858, connecting Trinity Bay, Newfoundland, with Valencia in Ireland, the *Strathroy Dispatch* was typical, if more than a little hyperbolic, in calling it the 'triumph of mind over matter, of light over darkness, of knowledge over ignorance, of truth over error, of science over space.' Its actual effects were less dramatic but perhaps more profound. It eliminated the necessity of the major papers to send their own correspondents to any but the most momentous and protracted news events, while at the same time giving small papers some of the benefits of large ones. It in fact permitted news to become a wholesale commodity as well as a retail one, though in Canada the wholesale dealers have often taken on the disguise of organizations very much like farmers' co-operatives. It made Canada both more British by making Britain seem close but also more American by making the shadow of America loom even larger across the map. It supposedly freed reporting of bias, but in fact merely standardized the bias, just as it standardized the prose. In other words, it further complicated the already complex relationship between newspapers and politics.

When the Reformers were swept into power in the Province of Canada in 1848, George Brown was on the threshold of a new era, when editors—which is to say proprietors as well, in many cases—emerged as social and political critics and added to publishing what was already enshrined in parliamentary practice, the idea of the loyal (rather than, as during the 1830s, disloyal) opposition. There was no more standing on the outside of power and events, banging for admittance. Even when an editor's party was not in power, his paper would have a recognized place in the social equation as a clearing-house for public opinion and a molder of it, a brokerage by means of which the public and the government might communicate with each other.

Editors were politicians by nature; in addition, some politicians were editors by trade. Francis Hincks, the founder in 1838 of the Toronto *Examiner*—who was premier of the united provinces of Canada between 1851 and 1854 and served as finance minister in the first Macdonald government after Confederation—is only one example. A list of others might include such newspapermen as William McDougall, founder of the Toronto *North American*, Michael Hamilton Foley, editor of the *Brantford Herald*, and D'Arcy McGee, founder of the Montreal *New Era*, all of whom also held various cabinet posts in the 1860s. McGee has special relevance for the way he used his paper as an engine of pro-Confederation sentiment, in somewhat the same manner as the Halifax *Novascotian* and the Montreal *Herald*, for example, were used for the opposing cause. McGee was born in Ireland, and his opposition to the Fenian movement caused him much trouble. After his last election victory in 1867 some of the Irish in Montreal roamed the streets seeking vengeance; the *Gazette*, which had endorsed him, feared attack, and the staff was prepared to take molten lead to the roof, if necessary, to pour it down on the protestors' heads.

It is difficult to know to what extent the politically minded editors of these and other papers were career journalists, sincerely bound up with the journalist's trade, or merely turned to journalism as so many turned to the law, to ease their way into political office and provide them with a livelihood once they left it. Joseph Howe of the *Novascotian* was of course a journalist first, at least during the earlier half of his long career. But there are relatively few cases like that of John Sheridan Hogan, who began as a youthful news-vendor (another career fostered by the advent of the steam engine and the penny press) and worked himself up through the printing trades to become a journalist and then the editor of the *British Colonist* in Toronto (which the Grand Trunk kept afloat on behalf of certain Tories until John A. Macdonald tried to sink it by helping to finance a rival, the *Daily News*). In 1857 Hogan was elected to Parliament, where he shared with McGee a reputation for great promise. But he was murdered by bandits in 1859. McGee, of course, was assassinated by a Fenian sympathizer in 1868. The crime was one of the events that proved the worth of the telegraph in spreading news quickly over wide areas to a public that was hungry for it.

Especially for editors, like George Brown, who believed themselves to be motivated by a high moral purpose (in this Brown was in the camp of his American contemporary Horace Greeley, though coincidentally so) the temptation to enter politics, and actually to make the changes one had been arguing for so shrilly, must have been irresistible. As early as 1851 Brown served in the Union parliament as an independent member after losing the Reform seat he sought to William Lyon Mackenzie, only recently returned from his exile; and in 1858 he joined with A.-A. Dorion to form the Brown-Dorion government, which lasted but two days. In 1864, as the leader of the Reform forces in Canada West, he put aside his intense personal differences with John A. Macdonald, leader of the Conservative element, to make workable the coalition that would lead to Confederation. In 1865, however, the tension between the two became unbearable and Brown resigned from cabinet. He stood for office in the first election in the new Dominion in 1867, but lost, and contented himself with being the power behind the scenes till the end of his days, which came in 1880, from the effects of a gunshot wound inflicted by a disgruntled former employee of the *Globe*.

At least five of the Fathers of Confederation were journalists. At the time of the Charlottetown Conference, however, only one paper beyond Prince Edward Island, the Saint John *Telegraph*, which was noted for its high ratio of hard fact to mere rhetoric, sent a reporter as such to cover the event. Brown, however, printed in the *Globe* the first draft of the British North America Act in February 1867, after receiving it by telegraph. But on the whole the interest of the press at this time took the form of argument rather than reportage. In Halifax, the *British Colonist* hailed the prospect of Confederation, whereas the *Chronicle* feared what the effect of the corresponding tariff would be; and the Quebec *Mercury* fretted that Quebec would lose its distinct identity if a union of the provinces were achieved. The *Free Press* in London, the *News* in Saint John, and both the *Herald* and *La Minerve* in Montreal, each thought the arrangement could make its respective city a far more important commercial and financial centre. As on virtually every other topic of the day, there was nothing if not an abundance of opinion.

3

WESTWARD EXPANSION

While the newspapers in eastern and central Canada were maturing in an atmosphere first of partisan manipulation and then of corporatism, those in the area now covered by Manitoba, Saskatchewan, Alberta, and British Columbia were being born. In many ways the pioneer West recreated some of the same conditions found in British North America in colonial times. As a result, newspapers underwent a process of development that was already familiar. They were published in remote areas, sometimes in the face of formidable commercial logic but always in answer to a social need, and were both nurtured and challenged by the pervasive nature of authority. Some were even tested by rebellion.

The rise of the press in the Hudson's Bay Company lands between the Pacific Ocean and Lake Superior began at both extremes more or less simultaneously, with several newspapers appearing at Fort Victoria on Vancouver Island in 1858 and another one at Fort Garry the following year. These events were of course unconnected, but in the 1880s newspapers began cropping up on the vast spaces between, appearing, as the towns themselves did, according to the advance of the Canadian Pacific Railway. As had been the case in Lower and Upper Canada some fifty years earlier, a printer or editor in one shop would go off to help create another establishment.

The first newspaper in the West was a French-language publication, *Le Corrier de la Nouvelle Caledonie journal politique et littéraire, organ des populations française dans les possessions anglaises*, two issues of which appeared at Victoria early in 1858, the work of one Paul de Gallo, who claimed to be a French nobleman and enjoyed the support of the Roman Catholic diocese. The paper was produced on a flatbed press that had come, through what travail can only be imagined, from France. When the venture failed, two Americans began a paper they first planned to call the *Anglo-American* but decided to name the *Victoria Gazette* instead, thereby admitting to a certain closeness to James (soon to be Sir James) Douglas, the Hudson's Bay Company governor who ran the colony of Vancouver Island and brooked no nonsense.

That winter a group of men met one night in a chemist shop in Yates Street to help a strange figure from Nova Scotia found a third paper, the *British Colonist*. The young man, who had grown up under the spell of Joseph Howe, was the former William Alexander Smith, who had taken the name Amor De Cosmos to show his love for humanity. Like a number of his contemporaries, De Cosmos (1825-97) took part in the California gold rush and then drifted northward when news came of fresh strikes along the Fraser River on the British Columbia mainland. His devotion to mining was short-lived; so, too, was his interest in photography, a new profession then, which he followed for a while. But he became a significant editor and politician.

The first issue of the *British Colonist*, a four-page weekly composed and printed in Wharf Street by De Gallo on his old French press, appeared in December 1858. Despite his later statement that he 'started the *Colonist* for amusement during the winter months', De Cosmos in fact had a strong political motive. He wished to set himself up in opposition to Governor Douglas, whose administration he was to criticize on the same grounds of privilege, favouritism, and nepotism that Mackenzie had laid at the Family Compact's door. In time De Cosmos arrived at three goals: to see the colonies of Vancouver Island and British Columbia united, and with responsible government, and, later, to see the resulting entity become part of Canada. Eventually he realized these ambitions and even became premier of the province, but he died a madman, shunned and mocked.

The Fraser gold rush, for which Victoria was the port of entry and supply depot, was supplanted by the Cariboo rush far to the north, and Victoria's population shrank dramatically. The first issue of the *Colonist* sold only about 200 copies. But the figure stood at 4,000 in 1862, by which time it had become a daily after an intermediate period as a triweekly. A new rotary press replaced De Gallo's flatbed press but was operated by manpower (the operator bore the colourful name Pegleg Larkin). A description survives of visitors having to pass through the composing room and pressroom in order to locate the editor's tiny office at the rear of the building.

Next to the Hudson's Bay Company itself, De Cosmos hated Americans most of all, and this stand made for perpetual controversy in a place based on gold-rush economics. It also ensured calumny from the owners of the *Gazette*, who once falsely accused De Cosmos of having sold shoes in San Francisco, a charge that calls to mind the slanderous assertion of rival pamphleteers that Daniel Defoe had dealt in (rather than manufactured) hosiery. De Cosmos was physically attacked more than once and would defend himself with his walking-stick.

In the frontier conditions of Victoria at the time, it was as though the telegraph, that essential tool of eastern journalists, did not exist, and the *Colonist*'s international news was inevitably spotty and stale. As though to compensate, or to underscore just where the readers' interests lay, the paper's local coverage was fulsome and aggressive, even to the point of taking petty developments in magistrates' court and blowing them up for comic affect, in the manner later associated with Bob Edwards and his Calgary *Eye Opener*. Of more substance were the political articles contributed by Charles Belford Young under the name 'Monitor', part of the long tradition of pseudonymous opinion that flourished throughout the nineteenth century, though usually only as expediency dictated.

On March 30, 1859, Governor Douglas reached the limit of his tolerance. Invoking an obsolescent English statute, he tried to suppress the *Colonist* by insisting that it post a cash bond of £800 as a promise of good behaviour. There is reason to suppose that De Cosmos could well afford that amount, but he suspended publication until April 9, by which time a groundswell of public support had built up, with readers contributing the money out of their own pockets. De Cosmos sold the paper in 1863.

The various early proprietors of the *Nor'-Wester*, the first newspaper published in the old North-West Territories, faced different obstacles. The two founders were William Buckingham, an Englishman, and William Coldwell (d. 1929?), a native Canadian, who resolved to commence a paper at the Red River Settlement (present-day Winnipeg), which in late 1858, when they arrived, had a population of 10,000. So isolated a place was it that the only other communities with which it was in direct and frequent communication were St Paul and other towns in Minnesota. Buckingham and Coldwell bought the Washington hand press said to have been used by the *St Paul Pioneer* in 1848. They then spent five weeks conveying it and other equipment, as well as a supply of books and stationery, to the Settlement. They travelled by ox cart, at the speed of 15 or 20 miles per day, and when they arrived, set up in a log house with a thatched roof. Rather grandly they called their business the Red River Printing and Bookselling Establishment.

Coldwell would remember that 'we had to become our own editors, reporters, compositors, pressmen, newsboys, and general delivery agents, besides having to undertake a house-to-house canvass throughout the entire settlement', selling subscriptions at 12/ sterling per annum, in advance. They 'met persons who assured us that they did not want the *Nor'-Wester*, because they knew more local news than we did; while as to the foreign news, they could learn as much as they desired from other papers which they got hold of at long intervals'.

The *St Paul Pioneer* had had a fire sometime in the early 1850s and the Washington press had fallen from the first floor to the ground floor, sustaining considerable damage, which a blacksmith had managed to reduce but never quite reverse. As a result, printing the *Nor'-Wester* proved especially laborious. But the first issue duly appeared on December 18, two sheets of 22 x 12 inches, with editorial and announcements commingled and the promise of 'secure reliable correspondence from Canada, St Paul and elsewhere' and of regular fortnightly publication. Within a few months, Buckingham gave up and took work at the Stratford *Beacon* in Canada West and was succeeded by James Ross, who in 1864 sold out his interest to Coldwell and went to Toronto, entering the employ of George Brown at the *Globe*. In 1865 fire destroyed the *Nor'-Wester*'s office and the stationery warehouse that adjoined it, and Coldwell decided to sell out and return east (but only for a while, as will be seen). The purchaser was Dr John (eventually Sir John) Schultz (1840-96), a non-practising physician who was the region's most important independent merchant (independent of the Hudson's Bay Company, that is).

Schultz was interested in using the publication to lash out against the company, though less for its autocratic rule than for its monopolistic business practices. He was neither an editor nor a printer, though he hired R.P. Meade as the former and George B. Winship as the latter. Winship was an American whom Schultz picked up in Saulk Center, Minnesota. Lured north with the promise of work, he found a room 12 feet square containing 'the crudest and most primitive collection of printing material that I ever saw, or have seen since in my rambles about the country.' Despite the aforementioned press, on which a full day was required to print the 400-copy run, Winship managed to add a note of professionalism, and indeed the *Nor'-Wester* switched to weekly publication. By means of a pony cart in summer and a dog-sled in winter, it was distributed over a wide area, reaching as far as Portage la Prairie, about 60 miles up the Assiniboine River.

In 1869, as the federal government was preparing to accept transfer of the entire North-West (Rupert's Land) from the Hudson's Bay Company, Dr Schultz sold the business (housed now in three small rooms rather than one) to Dr W.R. Brown, the local dentist, who kept on both Meade and Winship. Dr Brown refused to cave in to pressure from Louis Riel, whose reaction against the impeding change in the Red River's status reached the point of no return when he and his Métis militia seized Fort Garry, where he imprisoned Schultz and others. The Riel forces then took over the printing establishment, resolving to publish their own paper, the *New Nation*. As some material for the next issue of the *Nor'-Wester* was already made up on the stone, they simply used it, producing one issue of a queer dimorphic paper that was the *Nor'-Wester* on page one but became the *New Nation* on page three. Riel also intervened to prevent William Coldwell, who had now returned to the area, from carrying through with his plan for a new paper of his own, the *Red River Pioneer*. Dr Schultz, incidentally, escaped and made his way to Ontario, where he did much to agitate against Riel, a cause the overwhelmingly Protestant press of English Canada embraced with force and celerity.

One of the most heroic incidents in the Red River Rebellion came in July 1869 when Winship conspired with another printer, P.G. Laurie from Windsor, Ontario, to print secretly an anti-Riel proclamation. The fact that Winship 'was an American, neutral, and supposedly friendly' allowed him to smuggle type and ink out of the *Nor'-Wester* office, which was being used as a glasshouse. He recalled that 'it took us all the afternoon and most of the night to print 300 copies.'

Soon afterward, in January 1870, Major H.M. Robinson, having bought the press and type that Coldwell had brought from Ontario for his new venture, began publishing a newspaper for the benefit of Riel's provisional government, picking up the name *New Nation*. The paper stated its position thus: 'The Dominion Government, by its criminal blunders and gross injustice to this people have forever alienated them; and by their forfeiture of all right to our respect [whereas, by contrast, the] Imperial government we consider to be too far distant to intelligently administer our affairs [and so we believe that] the United States republic offers us today that system of government which would best promote order and progress in our midst, and open up rapidly a country of magnificent resources.' Later issues, as Winship stated, 'were devoted to the publication of reports of the Legislative Assembly [by Coldwell, its secretary, who was a fair phonographer, or shorthand reporter], to Riel's effusive addresses and Napoleonic proclamations, and to the diatribes against the Dominion officials.' When Riel retreated into exile for a time and the danger receded, Coldwell took control of the paper, aided by Robert Cunningham, the *Globe* correspondent there, and changed the name to the *Manitoban*. Other short-lived publications followed, including a French-language one, *Le Métis*, aimed of course at the Riel constituency. In 1872, the year that John A. Kenny and W.F. Luxton began what would be one of Canada's greatest journalistic enterprises, the *Manitoba Free Press*, a mob wrecked the *Manitoban*, the *Nor'-Wester*, and *Le Métis*. (Journalism, always a rough trade in the nineteenth century, was nowhere rougher than in the West. In 1886, when John W. Dafoe was in his first tour of duty as a reporter at the *Free Press*, the paper he would come to edit for forty-three years, he was threatened by a dog-fight promoter. The man had taken exception to the way Dafoe had described his business. Dafoe sought protection from the chief of police, who simply advised him to carry a revolver. Which he did.)

Patrick Gammie Laurie (1833-1903), the printer who helped Winship produce the anti-Riel broadsheet using type smuggled out of the *Nor'-Wester* shop, found that Riel had put a price on his head (£200), but he managed to escape across the American border. He was a Scot who had worked variously in Toronto, Cobourg, and Brantford as well as in the US, and who in the early 1850s had been proprietor of the Owen Sound *Sun* and later a Windsor paper, the *Essex Record*. Start-ups attracted him rather than daunted him. In 1878 he left Winnipeg with a press and type cases in an ox-cart, bound for Battleford. The town was then the capital of the North-West Territories and thus a place destined for growth and significance, a place moreover where government advertising and job printing might be picked up. As yet there was no printer there, nor anywhere else north of the international boundary between Winnipeg and Vancouver Island. He completed the 600-mile journey in 72 days to begin the fortnightly *Saskatchewan Herald*, with himself as reporter, compositor, printer, and bookbinder and, later, with his son R.C. Laurie to carry on after him. The paper, like the town, survived a devastating flood in 1884 and burning by Indians the following year.

The *Saskatchewan Herald* was the usual frontier paper: one sheet of four pages, four columns to the page, but with one curious difference traceable to local conditions. In the early days, before the railway reached Battleford, the freight on paper sent from Winnipeg was eight cents per pound and so, to permit as much matter as possible in the space available, the paper was set in 6 point type (72 points = one inch). When the transport situation improved, business picked up and paper prices fell, it became a five-column weekly, then an eight-page weekly set in 10 point. But during the recession of 1912-13 it would shrink in size and revert to 8 point type, eliciting complaints from farmers and ranchers who found it too difficult to read by the light of paraffin lamps.

Another instance of one newspaper contributing to the emergence of another came in 1880 when Frank Oliver (1853-1933) purchased a small job press and some old type from the *Manitoba Free Press*, supposedly for only $21, and took them by Red River cart to Edmonton, where he established the *Bulletin*, the first newspaper in what later became Alberta. He also took with him some of the politics of the *Free Press*, and would eventually serve in Laurier's cabinet as interior minister, continuing the immigration policies of his predecessor Sir Clifford Sifton, owner of the Winnipeg paper. In 1882 two other western newspapers were born, followed by four more in 1883.

Two former Mounties, E.T. Saunders and C.E.D. Wood (d. 1925), started the Macleod *Gazette* (by now the name had lost its official connotations) in September 1882 on a small Gordon jobber, a treadle-driven press commonly used to print handbills, letterheads, and the like. The result was the usual four-page, four-column paper, a trimonthly in the first instance, with a healthy ratio of local and general news to adverts, which came from Calgary as well from Montana, whence all goods derived until the CPR was operational. When they upgraded in 1884, for instance, their Campbell cylinder press came from Fort Benton, Montana, by steamer and then by cart; there was no steam power at Macleod to run it, however, and so it was operated manually by twelve Indians. The paper then changed to a six-column format, set in Brevies condensed. It closed in the early 1890s, succeeded by the Fort Macleod *Advance*.

The Prince Albert *Times* began in the same year as the town,

1882, with editorials contributed by members of the community as their way of supporting what everyone believed to be a much-needed enterprise. It was produced from a log cabin until moving eventually to the home of one of the proprietors. It was a Conservative paper unswervingly. But in the run-up to the general election of 1887 local Liberals started a sheet of their own, the *Critic*. The western and northern frontiers (wherever those lines of demarcation happened to be at any given time) had long been associated with primitive conditions for printing and publishing; one thinks of how the Rev. John Evans (1801-46), the Methodist missionary, rendered the Cree language into a syllabic alphabet at Norway House, 300 miles north of where Winnipeg would be one day, making type from old shell casings and printing books on birch-bark. In Prince Albert, forty years later, the publisher of the *Critic* wrote the text of the paper with a stylographic pen and impressed the sheet onto a bed of specially treated gelatin, creating a transfer by which a few duplicate copies at a time could be produced. One of the contributors was Clifford Sifton's brother Arthur, who was practising law in Prince Albert and later became premier of Alberta. The *Critic* eventually grew into the *Advocate*, which in time gave way to the *Herald.*

Calgary was the head of steel for the CPR when the *Herald* was launched there in 1883. Its full title at first was *The Calgary Weekly Herald, Mining and Ranch Advocate*. It was the usual four pages but of less than foolscap size, and was produced in a tent. But then in Calgary in 1883, with its population of 200 whites and perhaps twice that number of Sarcee, even the bishop's palace was a tent. The founders of the *Herald* were Thomas B. Braden (d. 1904) and Andrew M. Armour, both printers. When their first issue was to be published, in August, as part of the celebration of the arrival of the railway and the creation of the townsite, they mentioned to one of the visiting dignities, Mackenzie Bowell, MP, that they had not enough matter set in type to go ahead with publication. Thereupon Bowell, for years the proprietor and editor of the Belleville *Intelligencer*, rolled up his sleeves and went to work. Armour would remember, after Bowell became Sir Mackenzie Bowell, Canada's fifth prime minister, eleven years later, that he had been a 'whirlwind type slinger'.

Although all such first cries from the cradle should be treated skeptically, it is perhaps worth noting that in its première issue the Herald promised to expose 'all species of vice and immorality that come to our knowledge' and 'any measure or acts on the part of individuals, corporations or governments, which appear to be framed against the true interests of the place, people or district.' There were also the usual claims about advancing commercial interests and being 'thoroughly independent in the matter of politics'. As early as 1884 the *Herald* got some competition, from a paper called the *Nor'-Wester*, no relation to the former Winnipeg publication of the same name. The *Herald* denounced the *Nor'-Wester*'s editor as a 'childish egotist' and a 'lilliput from nowhere', announcing a long battle of invective of the sort that characterized the nineteenth-century press generally, and the western press in particular, and of which the public never seemed to weary.

Many such editorials were written by H.S. Cayley, a lawyer who became associated with the *Herald* early on and performed the literary function while Armour sold space. Cayley, who later became a judge in Vancouver, remembered that the 'one and only room of the establishment was also the typesetting room, the press room, and the wash room' and that 'our exchanges [were] confined to the Edmonton *Bulletin*, the Macleod *Gazette* and the stock journals of Montana, Idaho and Wyoming.' In 1885 he bought out Braden and Armour and made the paper into a daily, with a new press imported from Chicago.

Neither Armour nor Braden retired from the field, however. Armour had already moved to Medicine Hat, at the behest of the new town's citizenry, to edit the Medicine Hat *News*, which emitted weekly from one end of a disused boxcar donated by the CPR. It accelerated to daily frequency for two or three months before relapsing and assuming the alias the *Weekly Times*. He finally departed in 1886. A later editor was J.K. Drinnan (b. 1858), one of the Canadian *voyageurs* sent up the Nile to Khartoum in 1884 when Chinese Gordon, whom they arrived too late to save, was besieged there. He sold out in the early 1890s to another group of public-spirited citizens concerned about the viability of their newspaper, which then reverted to the name Medicine Hat *News*. It remained a weekly for years to come. As for Braden, once Cayley relinquished the *Herald* to two Winnipeg proprietors, who pursued a staunchly Tory line, he reappeared in Calgary to start the *Tribune*, which the *Herald* denounced as a 'venal sheet' run by a 'shameless libeller'. The *Tribune* closed in 1895.

One of the most extraordinary figures of the early western press was Nicholas Flood Davin (1843-1901), an Irish poet who from 1868 practised law in the Middle Temple prior to becoming a journalist in Fleet Street. As a war correspondent he was wounded during the Franco-Prussian conflict and used a hot-air balloon to make a daring escape from Paris during the Commune. He arrived in Toronto in 1872 to regain his health and went to work for the *Globe* and later for the *Globe*'s Conservative opposite number, the *Mail*. He thought to enter politics, but was defeated in the general election of 1878 in the riding of Haldiman (the same seat that Mackenzie had once snatched from George Brown). He practised a bit of law, his one important case being his unsuccessful attempt to save George Bennett from the gallows; Bennett was the former boiler-room attendant of the *Globe*, convicted of shooting Brown.

In 1883 Davin drifted west and determined to start the first newspaper in the District of Assiniboia, for at Regina, as at the other administrative centres in the new land, there was initially no shop to publish government advertising nor to undertake government printing. In November 1883 he floated one thousand shares of stock with a par value of $20, a level of capitalization not often reached by a weekly intended to serve a community of only 400 people. The money made a tangible difference, for although the *Leader*, as the paper was named, emanated from a small false-front building at Victoria Avenue and Rose Street, its equipment was far more elaborate and sophisticated than that usually to be found in such surroundings. In this as in other respects, Davin was thus favourably positioned to cover the Northwest Rebellion.

At first the eastern papers were not particularly alarmed by the news that Louis Riel had returned from exile in Montana to lead Métis and others in an uprising. But they made up for their indifference by reacting over-much after the rebels' initial victory at Duck Lake in the spring of 1885: 'Rebel Bonfires Light Up Saskatchewan Valley' was one headline in the Montreal *Daily Star*. But it is difficult to determine to what extent the press was the servant of the political mood and to what extent a contributor to it. To be sure the press, like the populace, quickly resolved itself along religious and linguistic lines, with Protestant English papers against Roman Catholic French ones. When the Dominion government sent a seven-thousand-man field force against Riel, the coverage was naturally fulsome.

Howard Angus Kennedy (d. 1930) was a reporter for the *Daily Witness*, the hysterically anti-Catholic paper in Montreal. He confessed to having no experience in war corresponding, only an admiration for a book called *Glimpses through the Cannon Smoke* by Archibald Forbes, who had covered the Russo-Turkish war for the *Daily News* of London, but he caused a sensation by interviewing Big Bear after the Frog Lake Massacre. 'My English whipcord riding suit, with knee-high boots, a Stetson hat; a spare flannel shirt, underwear and socks in my knapsack, with a wad of copy paper and bunch of pencils—that was my whole outfit', he would recall. That and a revolver. 'As most of the pioneer settlers in that region [near Battleford] had come from [Orange] rural Ontario, where the *Witness* was regarded with particular affection, I was most cordially welcomed by everyone.' The Montreal *Star* sent a staff correspondent as well, as indeed did *The Times* of London, for which paper Kennedy was to write in later years. But the *Globe* and the *Mail* in Toronto made do with the part-time services of two officers of the Queen's Own Rifles; such practices were common in the nineteenth century. At one point Kennedy visited P.G. Laurie at the *Saskatchewan Herald*. Laurie was forced to divide his time between military duties and the paper. Even so, he managed to produce two extras, one detailing the fighting at Cut Knife Hill, the other the decisive battle of Batoche. Revealing an early instance of the way that new technology eliminated as many advances as it brought about, Kennedy complained that some of his dispatches were pilfered by unscrupulous telegraphers or other parties.

Another writer associated with the Rebellion was William Bleasdell Cameron (1862-1951), whose book *The War Trail of Big Bear* was not published until 1926, with encouragement from Kennedy. But Cameron was not a correspondent in the Rebellion nor even a writer at that time; he was a trader at Battleford and Frog Lake who took up his pen only in the late 1890s, and later bought an Alberta weekly, the Bossano *Signal.*

Not unexpectedly, Davin proved by far the most able reporter of the journalistic corps, securing an exclusive interview with Riel on the very eve of his hanging in November 1885. He clearly won Riel's trust and indeed was sympathetic not only to a degree improbable for a Conservative (Davin would sit as a Tory MP from 1887 to 1900) but to an extent that an English journalist in the East probably would not have risked revealing. Speaking in French, Riel forgave his lawyers, saying: 'You were right to plead insanity, for assuredly all those days in which I have badly observed the Commandments of God were passed in insanity (*passé dans la folie*).' He sent more pointed messages to various politicians but respectfully thanked General Frederick Middleton for treating him well, saying to him through Davin: 'Pray see in my words the desire to be as little disagreeable as possible.' At some times Riel seemed less than rational. When he wound down, Davin asked him whether he had any more to add, and Riel replied that he had not. The next morning Davin set down a detailed stenographic account of the hanging, describing how the trap dropped as Riel was in the middle of reciting the Twenty-third Psalm. Davin committed suicide sixteen years later, after a full career in politics had succeeded his ones in law and journalism.

The Rebellion had important consequences for the editorial climate, to the extent that journalism could be separated from politics; it provided a focus for the religious divisions along which so much newspaper opinion was structured and indeed marketed. One dramatic example concerns the *News* in Toronto, an evening paper begun in 1881 by the Riordon family of St

Catharines, who had become wealthy and influential in the 1860s when they brought the process of mechanization to paper mills. In 1883 the paper had passed to Edmund E. Sheppard (1855-1924), a supporter of the Knights of Labour and other radical causes, who imbued it with flamboyance and enlightened sensationalism quite without precedent in the Canadian context (he even began printing on pink newsprint, anticipating the *Financial Times* of London by ten years). It was said that he had a special means of egress from the *News* building, enabling him to avoid writ-servers. But the tactic failed him when he was sued for libel by all the officers of the 65th Rifles of Montreal after he printed an allegation that the unit had shirked its duty in the Rebellion owing to religious and ethnic loyalties. At length he lost the case and also control of the paper, which reverted to the Riordons in 1887, whereupon Sheppard launched a new and totally different publication of his own, *Saturday Night*.

The western press continued its self-pollination. When in the year of the Rebellion the CPR created a townsite at Lethbridge, the Lethbridge *Herald* was one of the first businesses in the community, beginning in a shack behind the ironmonger's shop. E.T. (Si) Saunders (d. 1922), the founding editor, had worked with C.E.D. Wood at the Macleod *Gazette* and for the first year of publication he used the 'small army press' that the *Gazette* had imported so laboriously from Fort Benton; then he upgraded to a cylinder press, though it ran on horsepower before being adapted for petrol, then steam, and finally electricity. By 1905 the *Herald* had an up-to-date Monoline typesetting system as well as a daily edition called the *Southern Alberta News*, though the latter was comparatively short-lived. By then, the paper had long been edited by E. Hagel (d. 1930?), who had worked for Davin on the *Leader*.

As the western towns grew, they experienced the familiar proliferation of newspapers until each market reached the inevitable stage at which rationalization had to begin. From that point forward the western press began assuming much the same character as its eastern equivalent, a manner certainly different from that expected of newspapers today but fully consistent with the gradual realization that papers were tools of the political process and instruments of commerce. Those given to belief in the frontier newspapers as something more than that, or something different at least, suffered on in their own romanticism until the Klondike gold rush created new cities, or places very like cities, in the North. The *Yukon Midnight Sun* was the first paper to commence publication in Whitehorse, in 1898; it cost 50 cents per issue at a time when metropolitan papers in the south retailed at between one and five cents, depending on their class orientation and other market factors. Others followed: the *Klondike Nugget*, the *Klondike Miner*, and lastly the Whitehorse *Star*, which still survives and has been a daily or a weekly, according to the economic climate. The most renowned figure in the *Star*'s history was E.L. (Stroller) White (1859-1930), a tramp newsman, or boomer, who worked both sides of the Canada-US border and bore some resemblance to Bob Edwards of the Calgary *Eye Opener* as an exaggerator of news for comic effect and a vernacular literary figure. His fictional creations, used as a means of passing judgement on affairs of the day, included the Sam brothers, Flot and Jet.

Dawson had three daily newspapers during its gaudy heyday, and before the rush had petered out completely, one of them was using the latest Thorne Linotype. By 1909, however, only one of the papers, the *Daily News*, survived. In 1924 it retreated to the triweekly frequency so popular on the previous Canadian frontier a century earlier and in 1946 to weekly status; it closed after the territorial capital was moved to Whitehorse in 1951. There were still enough residents of Dawson to sustain a weekly, perhaps, but there was no longer the hope of government advertising, which had always made frontier papers feasible in the first instance and was second only to the railway as a factor in the development of the western and northwestern press.

Another distinctive feature of the western press were agricultural publications with mass appeal. By 1920 three of them, the *Nor'West Farmer*, the *Farmer's Advocate and Home Journal*, and the *Grain Growers' Guide*, were being produced in Winnipeg, and a fourth, *Farm and Ranch Review*, was coming out of

Calgary. Their combined circulation at the time was 231,000, and they served some of the same function as the religious papers by giving their readers a complete world-view while pretending to deal only with a narrow range of matters of interest to the particular group.

4

THE VICTORIAN ZENITH

In 1902 the engineer and educator Sir Sandford Fleming sponsored a competition for the best essay on the subject of journalism and the university, two institutions that were then not often spoken of together. 'The aim of the ordinary newspaper', wrote one of the respondents, W.D. LeSueur, a civil servant and historian who contributed regularly to the Montreal *Star*, 'is to be all things to all men.' So indeed it had come to seem. At their highest level of discourse, newspapers addressed particular constituencies. Such audiences were defined on the basis of religious criteria almost as often as on ideological ones. But on a quite different plane, newspapers were all trying to compete for the same readers. This represents a fundamental change in the press that came about slowly during the last three decades of the nineteenth century. The process can perhaps be illustrated by comparing the journalistic landscape of 1872 (a somewhat but not completely arbitrary date, as will be shown) with that of the turn of the century, approximately one generation later.

Whereas in colonial times papers were limited in number and circulation by factors as diverse as paper shortages and government interference, there seemed few such checks on growth in the late-Victorian period beyond those imposed by brutal economics. Canadian cities were growing rapidly, creating a new density of highly literate readers. Many newspapers scrambled for their attention; a few succeeded but many more did not. In 1872 there were slightly fewer than 50 daily newspapers in Canada; twenty years later the number had doubled. But the situation was more fluid than that statistic might suggest. Montreal, the biggest newspaper market in the country at the time, may be used as an illustration. Whereas Toronto, Halifax, and Saint John each supported four dailies, and Ottawa, Hamilton, and London had three each, Montreal in 1872 could boast four English-language dailies and three French. In the next thirty years, 23 other dailies began in Montreal and a total of 25 closed, including four of the original seven; on balance, the francophone press was less stable than the anglophone.

Newer cities, without Montreal's momentum, also became newspaper graveyards through the inexorable progress of mercantilism and laissez-faire economics. Fort William, Ontario, got its first newspaper of any sort, a handwritten affair called the *Perambulator*, in 1875; the cumulative tally stood at 16 papers at the turn of the century, by which time only one was then extant. In the adjoining community of Port Arthur the first newspaper, the *Thunderbolt*, also handwritten, was likewise started in 1875; by 1900 one strong daily, the *Chronicle*, dominated the market, having survived or absorbed 12 other papers of various frequencies.

This period between 1872 and 1900 saw not only the first great shake-out of the newspaper market but also the creation of the modern newspaper and thus the concept of the newspaper as what apologists sometimes call 'the daily miracle'. Tastes in design and typography have changed, due in part to advances in the means of production, but the modern reader would instantly recognize the newspaper of 1900, with its admixture of local, national, and world news, its clearly delineated editorial page, its abundant sports coverage, features, and columns, its letters from ordinary readers, and finally its classified sections and lavish display advertising.

In 1872 the daily circulation of the *Globe*, which stood at 18,000 in 1856 and 28,000 in 1861, had climbed to 45,000, making it the country's biggest. The latest spurt had been helped by George Brown's decision in 1868 to lower the price from $6 to $5 per annum while installing a new press with the capacity to address the increased sales that resulted. More than half his circulation was outside Toronto, which was just as well, given the degree of competition for urban readers, a situation that intensified in 1872 when the *Mail* was born, the result of the old antagonism between Brown and Sir John A. Macdonald. The *Globe*'s printers had struck and some had been jailed. Sir John was probably no more sympathetic to organized labour than Brown was, though he certainly was less strident on the subject. But such was his desire to damage Brown that his government pushed through the Trade Unions Act, legalizing unions. This same year, incidentally, the Conservatives were secretly supporting a labour weekly called the *Ontario Workman*, funnelling money to it through the postmaster-general in return for editorial endorsement, and at the same time withdrawing support from John Ross Robertson's Toronto *Telegraph*, which thus collapsed, forcing Robertson (1841-1918) to begin thinking about the *Telegram*, a paper that would always be Conservative without ever being a party organ in the old sense. Such was the atmosphere at the point where journalism and politics intersected.

Macdonald had been one of the young Conservatives who raised funds to launch the *Leader* to counterbalance the *Globe*. Unless they were actually politicians themselves, and increasingly such was not the case, the editors of party organs were prone to contract violent fits of political independence, and by 1872 Sir John had become disenchanted with the performance of the *Leader*'s publisher James Beaty. So the party abandoned the paper, which lingered until 1878 and is now remembered only in the name of Leader Lane, an alley that connects King and Wellington streets, west of Church. The Conservatives then passed the hat again in order to begin the *Mail*.

For all its technological innovation, the *Globe* remained in some respects the less modern of the two. Both were stridently partisan, of course, but the *Globe* extended the refuge of anonymity to ordinary readers, the sort whose letters-to-the-editor were beginning to reveal the complexity of the relationship between newspaper and citizen. The *Mail*, however, informed its readers: 'No notice can be taken of anonymous communications. Whatever is intended for insertion must be authenticated by the name and address of the writer; not necessarily for publication, but as a guarantee of good faith.'

Within five years the *Mail* was sold to its chief creditors, the paper magnate John Riordon and his family, who would come to hold equity in other Toronto dailies. The sale speaks not only of political fickleness but of overheads that climbed more quickly than technology could drag them down.

In 1864 most major papers paid 28 cents per lb. for paper. The Civil War in the United States so reduced the flow that shiploads of mummies were exported from Egypt to substitute for ordinary rags, which Canadian papers drew on exclusively at the time. Only after Confederation did chemical wood pulp begin to replace cloth in papermaking formulae, and the transition was slow. Halfway through the period under discussion, for example, a newspaper might be printed on a product that was 40 per cent rag, 40 per cent natural wood pulp, 10 per cent straw, and 10 per cent chemical wood pulp. As a result of this gradual change, the price of paper fell to an average of perhaps 12 cents per lb. by 1872 (and by 1900 would be only 2 cents). Yet the newspapers were physically big. The *Mail* of the 1870s was 22.5 by 30 inches, for instance, and the *Globe* at some periods was quite a bit larger, size being limited only by the breadth of a person's reach (and also perhaps by the genetic memory of the publishers, subconsciously remembering that until 1818 it had been illegal in England to publish newspapers greater than 22 by 33 inches).

Large pages plus big circulations spelled higher production costs, the fall in paper price notwithstanding. The story is told of how Hugh Graham (1848-1938), in the very early days of the Montreal *Star*, would rush into the street to sell newspapers in order to get enough cash to buy paper for the rest of the press run. He had begun work on the Montreal *Daily Telegraph* at 15 and founded the *Star* only six years later in partnership with another man whom he soon bought out. At first the paper was printed using steam diverted from the boiler room of a neighbouring building; when that source was cut off, a horse was used to turn the press. From those uncomplicated beginnings, Graham built an extraordinarily successful newspaper, based on belief in the Empire and his ability to supply the sort and the amount of news his audience desired. In time he became Lord Atholstan, the first press baron, in the literal sense, outside the mother country. One memoirist recounted Graham's instructions for printing the kind of copy that would tempt customers to read a story aloud to friends or family, and for many years no issue of the *Star* appeared without at least one item from Ireland, however trivial. By 1875 he had installed Canada's first web press to accommodate the rising circulation, which the following year was adjudged bigger than those of his three English rivals put together and by 1891 the biggest in Canada—for a time.

In contrast to the *Star*'s sympathy for Irish Catholics, who made up a sizeable proportion of the immigrant pool, the Montreal *Herald* was a Protestant paper, one with a strong commercial bias and a great deal of hard luck (through the late nineteenth and early twentieth centuries it suffered a series of disastrous fires, the last of which was the subject of one of Canada's first newsreels). Its more successful competitor, the *Witness*, daily since 1860, was zealously and narrow-mindedly evangelical; but its moral instruction notwithstanding, it was a complete and balanced popular newspaper, edited with skill, and informed by some guiding intelligence other than the Divine. It was the first Canadian newspaper to utilize its own newsboys to hawk papers in the streets, an admission not only that the old system of annual paid subscriptions had become inadequate as urban density had risen, but also that the news as a commodity had a shorter shelf-life than previously. In 1872 Montreal newsies were buying a dozen copies of the *Witness* at .66 of a cent per copy and retailing them at one cent each. The idea assumed variations as it gained currency. By 1875 the Quebec *Telegraph* had forsaken advance subscriptions in favour of sale to news agents (newsbrokers, in fact) who then employed their own army of youths. Thus began the Canadianization of the myth of the newsboy who makes good, a piece of folklore familiar to readers of Horatio Alger, one that would find its fullest expression in the anecdote about young John Diefenbaker selling a copy of the Saskatoon *Phoenix* to Sir Wilfrid Laurier in 1910.

At the point under review the francophone press was more

distinct from the anglophone than would be the case later on, but the price of singularity, in English eyes, was backwardness. English papers may have embraced religion, but only as one element of a political philosophy (e.g., the Orange Tories or the Methodist Liberals); their religious tone was often more a matter of opposition than of affirmation, more negative than positive, more hateful than tolerant. The French press, by comparison, was fulsomely sectarian. In the last days of 1871 *Le Pays* of Montreal had given up the struggle, much to the enrichment of *La Minerve*, which had a circulation of 5,000, carried a healthy mix of advertising to news and other editorial matter (about 60:40), and voiced the concerns of the old-guard Conservatives. But the mere fact that it was *bleu* rather than *rouge* was itself enough to worry the Bishop of Montreal and others, who felt that partisanship was being put before religious concerns. So it was that *Le Nouveau Monde* was begun in 1872 (the *Nouveau* was later dropped). It was a four-column evening paper selling for the usual $6 per annum, but it looked little like English papers that fit the same description. It forsook news as such—hot news, so infinitely malleable and marketable—sticking instead to the 'French front' style in which the first page was devoted to intricate argument or at least exposition, in a manner that had passed from fashion in the English press after the colonial period and the long twilight of Howe's *Novascotian*. In their choice of literary material, too, such papers were more serious, more likely to run instalments of Proudhon than of Dickens. The last example of the French front was said to be *La Patrie* of 1897, though ecclesiastical support of francophone papers was of course much longer-lived, as evidenced by clerical interest in *Le Droit* of Ottawa, begun in 1913. By then, however, French-language journalism had long since become more diverse in tone. The turning-point was the creation of Montreal's *La Presse*, a successful populist paper, in 1884. By 1900 its daily circulation would exceed even that of the Montreal *Star*—again, for a time.

Such were the outlines of Canadian daily journalism after Confederation. The papers of the next generation were quite different in appearance and content, and the changes bespoke far-reaching innovation in the business office, the editorial room, and the back shop.

One obvious shift was in the dimensions of the newspaper page, which began to shrink as a result of technological breakthroughs rather than of movement in the wholesale paper market. The central idea behind Richard Hoe's 'type-revolving machine', in which either the type itself or a matrix made an impression on the paper directly, finally came to the end of its long life. It was replaced with 'stereotyping', in which the type was used to make a mould from which a curved metal stereotype plate could be cast. The plate fitted on the drum of a press, which would be fed not individual sheets but a continuous spool of paper, or newsprint as it would come to be called in proto-Orwellian diction. Since the rolls of paper were mass-produced in mills, they were uniform in size, thus limiting the width of the finished newspaper to what could be achieved by trimming at the end of the production process. More important, though, was the fact that by passing the paper at high speeds between two such drums, each fitted with plates, both sides of the newspaper page might be printed at once, with little or no wasted motion. The cylinder press thus became a true rotary press, though it was still driven by steam or petrol until 1888, when the Vancouver *News-Advertiser* became the first newspaper in Canada to electrify such an operation.

News got newsier or more timely as the need to get it out quickly increased, and vice versa. Now such speed was greatly enhanced, and papers could go thicker as well. The eight-page paper soon replaced the four-page as the metropolitan standard and was itself soon superseded by the 12- or 16-page one. The trend towards bigger papers was partly the result, and partly the cause, of a climate for large display advertising and all manner of special editorial material. A few such innovations had begun in the 1870s but they did not gain momentum until the 1890s, by which time the last great obstacle—the problem of how to set type more quickly—was finally being overcome.

For years, inventors and entrepreneurs had been trying to address the question of automated typesetting. Various machines (such as the one on which Mark Twain lost his fortune) were found wanting, usually because they tried to pluck existing type from a bank or tray at high speeds and broke down under the weight of their own convoluted movement. Ottmar Mergenthaler (1854-99), a German-born typesetter in the US, approached the matter differently, creating a keyboard that was connected to matrices that drew on a ready supply of molten lead to cast each character as needed, producing complete lines of type, one-column wide, which accumulated automatically in a receptacle like a compositor's stick, ready to be transferred to the *forme*. The Linotype, as it was called, became available in the 1880s and 1890s and had to compete with several rival systems. Both the *Chronicle* and the *Telegraph* in Quebec and *La Patrie* in Montreal favoured the 'Monoline' at first, and the editor of the Ottawa *Journal* would later confess his error in opting for 'Typographs' at $1,500 each before replacing them with Linotypes at twice the price. And bigger papers of course needed more machines, great long banks of them, the Montreal *Star* purchasing 14 in 1898, by which time *La Presse* already had a dozen in operation.

One side-effect of the Linotype, particularly once the price came down, was to suddenly give the smallest weekly the means to set as much copy as it could possibly need. This spelled the end of the several companies that syndicated 'readyprint' matter, finished pages that country publishers could pass off as the products of their own shops.

Throughout this period successively more advanced models were introduced and all proved their worth in ways both obvious and subtle. The Linotype cut the cost of composition at least in half (to 14-15 cents per 1,000 ems in the case of the Ottawa *Journal*, for example). Relative ease of operation meant that trained printers would no longer enjoy the monopoly on typesetting that had been forced on them by the steam-driven press so long before. In at least two cases, at the *Citizen* in Ottawa and the *News-Advertiser* in Vancouver, strikers were unable to shut down their papers after non-union labour was brought in to operate the Linotypes.

The other great transformation of this period, one more obvious to the reader, was the introduction of photographs, which doomed the honourable profession of newspaper sketch-artist and gave enormous aid to the Victorian assumption that newspapers were not only transcriptions of absolute reality but represented the Truth. Like the other new mechanical processes, this one came about slowly, but unlike the others it could boast of Canadian origins. Georges Edouard Desbarats (1838-93) briefly held the post of Queen's Printer, which his father, after a career with the Quebec *Mercury*, had had before him. In 1869 Desbarats established the *Canadian Illustrated News*, which in 1871 became the first newspaper to publish a photograph—a view of the new Custom House in Montreal. But he and his partner, William Leggo, spent years perfecting their invention and proving its practicality. Later they began a newspaper in New York called the *Daily Graphic*, which was not only the first daily tabloid newspaper in the US, of the sort made feasible by the spread of public transportation, but on December 2, 1873, became the first paper to publish what would soon be the staple of newspaper make-up, a halftone photo-engraving (a view, in this case, of Steinway Hall). The facts seem beyond dispute, though most sources contend that the feat was first achieved in 1880, with a halftone of a hobo shantytown. In any case the process took years to spread. The first such picture in a Canadian daily newspaper was a portrait of Sir Wilfrid Laurier in the Saturday *Globe* of March 28, 1891, three weeks after the general election (it caused a sensation). Very shortly afterward came one showing Sir John A. Macdonald's vacant office; it was received with emotion by people mourning his death. By that time the *Daily Graphic* had folded (1889), but Desbarats had two other publications back in Canada, *L'Opinion Publique* and the *Dominion Illustrated* (the *Canadian Illustrated News* had ceased publication in December 1883). Another half-generation would pass before halftones overwhelmed the daily newspaper industry as a whole. Until then their use was confined to large papers whose publishers utilized them as part of complicated marketing strategies aimed at attracting the most readers not through the promotion of one essential product but through the skilful juggling of numerous variants.

Morning and evening papers were perceived as different species of beast, the former of greater interest to the middle-class, the latter to the lower middle-class and to working people. The telegraph both strengthened this division, by giving AM papers the benefit of national and foreign transmissions that built up overnight, and weakened it, by providing PMs with the opportunity to beat morning papers on fast-breaking events of the afternoon, when most politician happenings, for example, became known. Also, the creation of various categories of news favoured one or the other. For example, as Canadian stock markets became more important after Confederation (a development reflected in the founding of the Toronto *Monetary Times* in 1867 and the Montreal *Journal of Commerce* in 1875), the advantage was given to the PMs. Conversely, the rise of professional spectator sports, with the seasonal schedules and complex intercity rivalries, favoured the AMs, particularly once night games became popular later on. Accordingly, in the 1870s both the *Globe* and the *Mail* were producing three-cent evening editions to take advantage of what proved to be only temporary opportunities in the marketplace, while in the 1880s the Toronto *World*, a one-cent popular (even radical) paper, changed from nocturnal to early-morning habits, hoping to out-manoeuvre its competition. As late as 1900 the London *Free Press* would echo ancient wisdom in claiming to reach 'the classes with the morning [edition], the farmers with the noon, and the masses with the evening....' Other publishers might produce second papers under separate names. Thus in Halifax in 1880, the *Mail* (Tory) and the *Echo* (Liberal) were in reality the morning editions of the evening *Herald* and the evening *Chronicle* respectively. The following decade, the *Manitoba Free Press* offered free subscriptions to its evening *Bulletin* in an attempt to erode the base of the city's other evening paper, the *Telegram*.

Weekly editions added to the confusion. In the 1870s the major papers were still producing weekly digests for rural subscribers, with type that had been set and used during the preceding seven days but with original material as well, including copy of specific agricultural interest. Such papers were characteristically in a different format from their daily counterparts; in 1873, for example, the weekly *Globe*, which came out Friday mornings and was priced at $2 per year as opposed to $5 for the daily, measured 20 by 30 inches; by 1879 it had assumed almost tabloid proportions. In a number of venues such editions evolved into weekly magazines for the provincial readership: the *Family Herald* (founded in 1869) of the Montreal *Star*, the *Free Press Prairie Farmer* (1872) of the *Manitoba Free Press*, the *Star Weekly* (1910) of the Toronto *Star*, though the last of these was less rural than the others, seeking instead a general family market nationwide. In any case, photographs at the turn of the century were still a visual luxury usually reserved for such weekly or weekend editions, with their better-quality paper and the greater hospitality they showed to feature material. Take the case of the Toronto *Sunday World* (which in fact had to be printed and distributed on Saturday to avoid violation of the law). It was an eight-page paper costing five cents; in 1895 the front page was seven columns of grey type relieved by a few small headlines and an editorial cartoon above the fold; in 1905 the page was eight columns wide, showed evidence of typographic design, and was decorated with large, silvery photographs of people and locations. The first action photograph in a Canadian newspaper came the following year when a shot of horses competing in the King's Plate appeared in the London *Free Press*. It was taken by the proprietor himself, Arthur Blackburn, who had introduced the Linotype and other innovations to the paper, which has been in the Blackburn family since 1852. In 1900, though, only a few papers had the capacity to reproduce photos, and of those that did, even news events of enormous importance might not justify such usage. The ideal case in point is the Boer War, in which Canadian troops were participating thanks largely to the efforts of the Montreal *Daily Star*, which had promoted the conflict as one of its famous causes (as it would later promote inoculation against smallpox) even to the extent that the proprietor personally insured the lives of Canadian soldiers. The war was soon consuming the public's attention as few events outside the country had ever done, but the Brantford *Expositor* was typical when, in devoting its whole front page to the relief of Mafeking, it used as illustration a sketch of Baden-

Powell and a crudely drawn map. Nor was the Edmonton *Evening Journal* able to use a photograph on September 2, 1905, when Alberta became a province; all the space above the front-page fold was unrelieved type, and all the space below, display ads. Yet by the First World War the photograph was ubiquitous if only on a local level, for the telegraphic transmission of such images had yet to be perfected. By the 1920s only the Montreal *Gazette* was conspicuously, almost absurdly, old-fashioned in its resistance to them.

Telephones helped to change the newspapers as well, not leastwise by catering to the incessant clamour of short deadlines and also by undermining the formal nature of the news interview, reducing it to the level of impressionism and eliminating the emphasis on completeness and stenographic accuracy that had characterized the form in the 1870s. By 1890 the 'news room' (in former times a reading-room or subscriber-backed private library, but now the room in which editorial functions were performed) might have one communal telephone mounted on the wall, whereas by 1900 the Toronto *World*, for example, made a point of displaying its telephone number on the masthead.

Another contributor to the mechanizing and modernization of the newspaper was the typewriting machine ('typewriter' referred originally to the operator, not to the device itself). As news copy was disposable once it was printed, it is difficult to trace the spread of this particular technology in Canadian journalism. Perhaps it is of some value to note that the oldest typewritten government document in the National Archives is an order-in-council dated 1886. Cora Hind (1861-1942), who would become famous both as a leader of the woman's suffrage movement and as the crop prognosticator of the Winnipeg *Free Press*, was first refused work at the paper in 1882 because of her gender, even though she had recently qualified as a typewriter-operator, one of the few such persons west of the Lakehead, if not indeed the only one. But no doubt the rebuff is less a commentary on technology than on the place of women in journalism, which was also undergoing remarkable change in the period being looked at.

The umbrella term sometimes used for the editorial environment created by metropolitan publishers in the late-Victorian era was 'personal journalism', by which was meant a new freedom to pursue the all-things-to-all-people attitude and with it, perhaps, commercial success. Another phrase was 'new journalism' (which resurfaces from time to time, though Tom Wolfe's definition was as different from H.L Mencken's as Mencken's had been from Matthew Arnold's). Both usages signified an eyewitness approach to news at all levels, a willingness to promote celebrity and a compartmentalizing of the paper, with sections aimed at particular segments of the total readership. Women were one such special audience. The *Globe* pioneered a women's page in 1882, one fleshed out with syndicated material from the US, but it never achieved the popularity of the 'Women's Kingdom' column and related features found in the *Mail* in 1889 and continued in its successor, the *Mail and Empire*, from 1895. The page was conducted by Kathleen Blake Coleman (1864-1915), known as 'Kit' or 'Kit of the *Mail*', who grew to be one of the best-known journalists of the time, particularly after she schemed to become the only accredited female correspondent in the Spanish-American War, 'by no means either a pleasant or glorious occupation.' One of the first female journalists in Canada and one of the most significant was Sara Jeanette Duncan (1861-1922), a native of Brantford, who between 1885 and 1889 held important positions, as leader writer and political correspondent, with the Washington *Post*, the Toronto *Globe*, and the Montreal *Star* in turn, later devoting her talent to works of fiction, including, most famously, *The Imperialist* (1904).

At the close of the Victorian era some important newspapers, such as the Saint John *Sun*, the Toronto *Telegram*, and the *Manitoba Free Press*, resisted columns as such, no matter what the targeted audience, but they were the exceptions. Columns could be serious or trivial. Some anglophone papers used this mechanism to cover British politics, while *La Patrie* ran a 'Courrier de France' on its front page every day. Material aimed at women was likely to take column form as well; much of it was concerned with domestic and child-rearing matters, or with fashion. The Montreal *Herald* of the 1890s ran a complete menu each day with relevant recipes. Kit Coleman was not the only women's-page editor to build a slavish following for such writing (another was her contemporary Robertine Barry of *La Patrie*, who wrote as 'Françoise'). No such apprenticeship in the shop of preconceived ideas was necessary for the feminist and reformer Emily Murphy (1868-1933) who, though not a staff reporter on any one paper, contributed regularly to many until her pseudonym, 'Janey Canuck', became instantly recognizable. Overall, though, women's progress in the newsrooms was slow, allowing even for the later vogue for 'sob sisters' to wrestle with the human-interest side of sensational stories. Gwen Cash English insisted that when she was hired by the Vancouver *Daily Province* in 1917 she became the first full-time female reporter in Canada to be assigned a general beat of the sort overseen by a city desk—that is, a beat normally covered by males; the claim seems bold, but the underlying point is certainly real enough. It goes without saying that women were paid less than men even in an age when reporting was almost synonymous with poverty, when Sir John Willison could remark that journalism 'is not exactly a profession, not exactly a trade, not always a means of livelihood'.

Several of the largest and most self-important newspapers of the 1890s, such as the Toronto *Globe* and the Montreal *Star*, erected new buildings for themselves during that decade, hoping that the structures would become instant landmarks; the Toronto *Mail* actually modelled its own after the Pulitzer Building in New York. Salaries and also the number of staff were slow to reflect these new realities, though such sluggishness was also related to the pace of technology. To note that in 1878 the Montreal *Witness* had the same number of editorial employees (13) as it had employees in its job shop is to know either that its job shop was extraordinarily busy or that labour-saving machines had not made much of an inroad there. Credence is lent to the second conclusion by the fact that the paper at that time had 15 pressmen and 35 compositors, for this was before the Linotype and the rotary presses. A corollary of this is that the size of the editorial department did not necessarily determine its quality. *La Presse* in the late 1880s had only four editorial employees. As late as the 1920s, at the height of its national and international renown, the *Manitoba Free Press* had not only one of the grandest newspaper buildings but one of the lowest salary scales for its staff of only 50.

In the 1870s reporters might earn no more than average workingmen in industry, perhaps a dollar per day. In the 1880s and 1890s they might work a 62-hour week for between $500 to $600 per annum, with the most experienced people paid at perhaps twice that rate, especially in the large cities. Wages for craft workers were comparable. Counting everyone from the publisher to the porter and half a dozen apprentices, the Toronto *Telegram* had a staff of 80 in 1898 (as compared with more than 500 when it ceased publication in 1971). The total included 12 persons in the business office, 17 in editorial, 26 in the composing room, four in the press room and three in the stereotyping room. Fully one-third of them were earning $20-21 per week. But reputation, whether the employee's or the newspaper's, was not an absolute guarantee of high rewards. Kit Coleman left the *Mail and Empire* in 1911 when asked to provide, in addition to her other duties, a daily column for the front-page with no increase in her salary of $35 per week, which had remained constant for years (an injustice that twenty-five years later still irritated J.V. McAree, the *Mail and Empire* and then *Globe and Mail* columnist). She promptly resigned and began a column that she syndicated herself to a dozen other papers, which each paid her $5 per week.

Nor in the mid-Victorian period were editors themselves given exceptional rewards. Proprietors found it more difficult to acquire true wealth than political power, but some succeeded in the first goal. George Brown of the *Globe* would occupy a substantial mansion in Toronto's Beverley Street, and John Ross Robertson of the *Telegram* would have an equivalent house in Sherbourne Street at the other end of the downtown era. But in 1882, the period between Brown's death and Robertson's peak, George Johnson, the editor (rather than the proprietor) of the same city's *Evening News*, moved into the newest house of a long terrace in Beverley Street whose other residents included a solicitor but also a tax collector, a salesman, even a barber—strictly middle-class. The salary gap between editor and reporter, however, could only widen as the editor's job came to be seen as a management position, and a few editors, such as T.C. Patteson of the *Mail*, Joseph Atkinson of the Toronto *Star*, and Walter Nichol of the Vancouver *Province*, were able to purchase control of their own papers when they found politically astute bankers or capitalists willing to back them. No other Canadian proprietor, by the way, quite reached the same level of conspicuous wealth as Lord Atholstan of Montreal, who by 1900 had built a magnificent seven-storey mansion at the corner of Sherbrooke and Stanley streets, a block or two from Mount Royal.

As to what was considered appropriate background and training for a journalist, here again there is a distinct difference between the practice of French Canada and that of English Canada. There were always a few eccentrics with improbable pasts that were nonetheless true, such as Edmund E. Sheppard of the Toronto *News,* who had been a stagecoach driver in the American Southwest, or Honoré Beaugrand of *La Patrie*, who had fought in Mexico with the troops of the Emperor Maximilian. Generally speaking, Quebec editors were more likely to be trained for the law than their English counterparts, as was the case with the Conservative power-broker C.-A. Danséreau of *La Minerve* and later *La Presse*, to take only the most conspicuous example. The education level of lesser editorial employees also tended to be higher in francophone than in anglophone journalism, which counted university graduates as relative rarities well into the twentieth century. English-Canadian journalists clung to the romantic fiction that they were members of the printing trades (rather than members of the advertising profession). In fact each wave of technological progress raised another barrier between the mechanical tradesmen and those who worked with their hands only by means of a pencil. Apprentices in the back shop could no longer cross over to editorial work, which left editorial employees to transfer their elaborate sympathy to the copyboys, lads who spirited copy from the editorial room to the composing room, which might be in a different building, or from the various bureaus to the main office. In the folklore of the profession, copyboys would proceed inexorably to be cub reporters or 'cadets', as the phrase then was. Once established, they might begin on the hotel beat, as the young John W. Dafoe did in 1883 when he joined Hugh Graham's staff of seven on the Montreal *Star*, checking the registers for newsworthy travellers who might suffer themselves to be interviewed. From there one could progress through police news and court news to political reportage, if not diverted along the way into a job such as telegraph editor. In French-speaking Quebec, by contrast, the beat system was unknown until its adoption by *La Presse* in 1900.

The French-language press also had more respect for literary achievement than did its English-language counterpart. Lorne Pierce, the book publisher, noted that more than half of the 82 writers in Jules Fournier's seminal collection *Anthologie des poètes canadiens* had journalistic pedigrees. Henri Bourassa would prove particularly adept at hiring literary people to work at *Le Devoir*. Both cultures, however, shared in the practice of letting writers support themselves through patronage appointments in the civil service, a tradition that sometimes overlapped with journalism, most notably in 1892-3 when the poets and civil servants Wilfred Campbell, Archibald Lampman, and Duncan Campbell Scott alternately wrote the 'At the Mermaid Inn' column in the *Globe*. Another aspect of journalism, one that found expression in the founding of press clubs in the 1890s, was the note of sometimes self-conscious literary or artistic bohemianism, as voiced, for example, in the life of Bernard McEvoy of Toronto (1842-1934?), the author of such books as *Away from Newspaperdom and other poems* (1897), or in that of John Reade (1837-1919), who was literary editor of the Montreal *Gazette* for the last forty years of his life and for most of that time had no equivalent elsewhere in the press. The pleasant self-delusion that one was a terribly worldly artist of sorts rather than a chairbound trivializer—a view held by many more-or-less footloose reporters—was more easily maintained in the age before unionized newsrooms and a university-driven sense of career mandate. Daily journalism as distinct from advertising was even less hospitable to Canadian visual artists, though C.W. Jefferys was made chief illustrator of the Toronto *Daily Star* in

1905 and art director of the *Star Weekly* in 1910.

Although the Linotype made setting type faster and easier, it robbed the process of much of its humanity, and in the 1890s newspaper prose began to lose its Victorian tumescence. Another reason for the change, of course, was the sheer plurality of the audience. The newspaper that aspired to be all things to all people must perforce be intelligible to everyone, and by 1900 immigrants were looking to the dailies for instruction in mastering English. As early as the early 1880s, Edmund E. Sheppard was introducing to the Toronto *News* the concept of the sentence-paragraph, a rhetorical structure traceable all the way back to Defoe but one not previously considered suitable for newswriting as such. By 1900 the Toronto *World* had procedures in place for exhorting reporters to write with childlike simplicity from a standpoint that was both impersonal and non-referential. At this period news stories were not usually signed except in extraordinary circumstances. Indeed, the fashion demanded that even columns of opinion appear under initials only or some *nom de plume* rich in literary significance, a tradition that seems to have lasted longest at the Winnipeg *Free Press*, where the *Manchester Guardian* was almost as influential as the Manchester School. From 1911 on, readers of the rival *Tribune* could find the veteran political journalist and poet W.T. Allison (1874-1941) writing literary articles as 'Ivanhoe'. Not all papers were so bookish or even so literate. By-lines became increasingly common after the First World War, as rewards for exemplary service or acknowledgement of some special expertise. At length, reporters came to expect them as a right. Proprietors were perhaps happy to allow this presumption to flourish as it weakened the sometimes awkward notion that the owner was personally liable for whatever the institution might publish. The parallel with the principle of responsible government and its erosion by creeping republicanism is of course obvious.

The final important change in the face of Canadian daily journalism between the 1870s and the 1890s was the newspaper's rise as an advertising medium. In the 1870s classified advertising ('small adverts') was virtually the only kind available. The

Toronto *Telegram*, for instance, built its early success on penny-a-line want ads. The advantage to the publisher was that there was no more lucrative way to sell a page than to split it up into a hundred or more small units that were paid for in advance, though it might be difficult to generate a steady flow of new accounts as older ones expired. In 1889 one-sixth of the Toronto *Mail*'s Saturday edition consisted of such notices. But attention was beginning to focus on 'departmental stores', which sold each product in volume and at one inviolable price much below that of the traditional dry-goods merchant. As such stores grew in the 1880s under Timothy Eaton, Robert Simpson, and others, they changed the publishing climate. Whereas previously newspapers had depended on modest national ads of a more or less permanent nature, such as those that touted patent medicines, and on even smaller local ones that might be valid for only a short period of time or, like steamboat schedules, varied from week to week, now there was need for the new-style local merchants, with their mammoth downtown stores, to buy large ads—typically a half-page or multiples of a half-page—to advertise the bargains peculiar to that day or a few days. This new arrangement proved lucrative for everyone concerned. By the 1890s metropolitan dailies were deriving only one-third of their revenues from subscriptions and single-copy sales. To manage the purchase of such advertising in bulk, and to orchestrate national campaigns for particular products, there arose a new type of establishment, the advertising agency. The Montreal firm headed by Anson McKim was the best known. With the introduction of middlemen like McKim, a newspaper's advertising rate card often became a suggestion rather than a proclamation, and such factors as the extent of paid circulation, as well as its exact composition, took on vital importance. In 1895 an agency could buy a one-time full-page ad in the Ottawa *Journal* for $45, or two cents per agate line, whereas the same ad in the Montreal *Star* would be five cents per agate line even with a substantial discount for multiple insertions. The presence of the agencies also meant the im-mediate improvement in the visual side of advertising, though in this they were merely instruments of the modern consumerism and its demands.

Department stores and other foundations of this new type of commerce could guarantee the existence of a newspaper that might not otherwise survive. To publications already well established, they were a wonderful boost. Eaton's began purchasing full-page ads in the *Free Press* each day from almost the instant it opened its Winnipeg store in 1905. But this power gave the merchants a weapon with which to threaten publishers. In 1900 Henry Morgan & Co. cancelled its advertising in the Montreal *Star* and *La Patrie*, which it accused of stirring up animosity between the two founding races. As late as 1921 Sir John Eaton tried to force the Toronto *Daily Star* to ameliorate its views on social democracy by withdrawing his advertising for a year. Such censorship could be more worrisome than the threat of libel, which was quite worrisome enough. In the next generation the Eaton family went so far as to finance a new proprietor's purchase of the *Star*'s adversary, the *Telegram*.

5

THE LIFE AND DEATH OF THE PARTY PRESS

One of the reasons newspapers grew numerous in the 1830s and 1840s was the perceived need for both a Tory publication and a Reform one in every important population centre so that each could check the outrages of the others. Early newspapers were powerful weapons in a perpetual battle but they were not necessarily implements of public opinion as later ones were, for they most often preached to the converted. People subscribed (in both senses of the term) only to that paper which supported, and was supported by, the political party to which they felt passionate allegiance.

Newspapers, all newspapers, were narrow and sectarian in political matters to an extent wholly unfathomable today, and readers grew accustomed to their being so; they learned to make allowance for windage and partisan hyperbole. In fact, members of the public seemed to wear their papers as they would badges, and became quite caught up in the incessant bickering and squabbling amongst rival publications. Thus the origin of Canada's party press, which, after responsible government itself, was perhaps the second most influential idea to emerge from the troubles of the 1830s. It was one that had a tremendous impact on Canadian life and politics through the remainder of the nineteenth century and for a surprisingly long time during the twentieth as well.

Writing in the 1940s, Arthur Ford, the long-serving editor of the London *Free Press*, recalled his early days in Winnipeg and Ottawa when 'A Conservative paper covered the speeches of its leaders and more or less ignored the speeches of the Liberals and vice versa. Reporters were biased and unfair . . . government news was treated like patronage for the government papers. It was one way a grateful ministry paid newspapers for support. Opposition papers could obtain any government news only through the kindness of friendly correspondents or through underground sources.' As early as the 1860s the federal Conservatives were spending $100,000 per year, a considerable sum, on the purchase of favourable newspaper treatment. The Conservatives are named here for no other reason than that it was they who were in power at the time the estimate was made: no one party was at bottom any more, or less, guilty in this matter than another. Such at least was one face of a complex kind of symbiosis, as sincere as it was corrupt, that warrants a more thorough examination.

Behind every successful politician was a newspaper doing his dirty work; behind every proprietor or editor, a politician, or group of politicians, offering support (if only temporarily, as expediency might dictate). Because Sir John A. Macdonald's personality and career are such common currency, one can turn to him for illustrative purposes once again. Macdonald exhibited a sharp interest in newspapers that might be able to curb the influence of Brown's *Globe*. Beginning in 1852 his brightest hope was the Toronto *Leader*, the most important in a succession of papers owned by James Beaty (1798-1892), a Toronto leather merchant and financier, who retained Charles Lindsey (1820-1908) to edit it for him. In Macdonald's correspondence we find the politician tipping off Lindsey in January 1858 that 'The House, or rather Parliament meets for the dispatch of business on Thursday the 25th February. The [Canada] Gazette will contain this officially', at which point the other papers would hear of it for the first time if there were no other leaks in the interim. Before the end of the month Macdonald is boldly giving orders on how another, far more important, scoop should be treated. 'Announce tomorrow that Ottawa has been selected by the Queen as the future seat of Govt.', he writes. 'Do not say anything about any action of the Govt on the matter. I need not say that it should go in at the *last* moment, to prevent the Globe having it in the morning.' In 1867 Lindsey was rewarded for years of labour by being made registrar of deeds in Toronto. He was thus no longer in the editor's chair when Sir John withdrew support from the *Leader*.

In 1872, dissatisfied with much of the Tory press for its weak performance generally, Sir John canvassed his allies for money, and urged them to canvass still others, in order to found what came to be called the *Mail*. At the outset the *Mail* boasted that it was to be a general-interest newspaper, not simply a political news-sheet, and that it would maintain an independent conscience. But these had become *pro forma* assurances. The prospect of the *Mail* at first delighted Goldwin Smith (1823-1910), the former Oxford don and the very image of Victorian liberalism who was already, at this early stage of his life in Canada, the most prominent intellectual figure in the Dominion. Although he never stood for office, he was ever the keen observer and critic of Canada's politics and way of life, even though he always claimed to be no more than an objective bystander (*The Bystander* being the name of one of the many periodicals in which he had a hand over the years). He was a fierce moral and social force, a bigot where women and minorities were concerned, a foe of imperialism, and a champion of Irish Home Rule. He was also a denouncer of strictly partisan journalism, in contrast with what he saw as the 'polyantagonistic' brand he himself practised. As such he quickly became disappointed with the *Mail* when, the following year, it abandoned its show of independence within the Conservative ranks and began a daily defence of Macdonald's actions in the Pacific Scandal.

There were now two Tory newspapers arrayed against the *Globe*, and so in 1875 the Liberal politician Edward Blake decided to begin another paper to represent the other side. He called it the *Liberal*, straightforwardly enough; but like so many Victorian politicians, he revealed his true devotion to journalism in the abstract by scrapping the paper shortly thereafter, in order to accept a post in Alexander Mackenzie's cabinet. At about this time, Smith, who already had private means and had married a wealthy Toronto widow (to whose mansion he had added a wing for his library), assisted with the initial funding for the Toronto *Telegram*. Later still he would help to back the *Tribune* in Winnipeg. Questioned about his apparently indiscriminate generosity to such ventures, he once remarked that he would have used the money for a yacht but would not have had nearly so much fun.

As time wore on and Macdonald's political fortunes waxed and waned, the *Mail*, too, began asserting its independence, and this gave the edge to Smith, who was evolving his views on political and economic union with the United States, views that culminated in 1891 in his infamous book *Canada and the Canadian Question*. He began to write unsigned editorials for the *Mail* and almost succeeded for a time in making it a totally continentalist paper. For Macdonald that was the last straw. In 1887 he passed the hat amongst the party faithful again to finance another new Conservative morning paper, one that might balance out the infidel *Mail* and the renegade *Telegram*, which themselves were supposed to be restraining the *Globe*'s perniciousness. The new venture was called the *Empire* and this time there would be no slip-ups. Hector Charlesworth, who once worked on it, would call the *Empire* 'as far as I know, the first Canadian newspaper to be, in the completest sense, party-owned and party-controlled. . . .' Which of course it was not, not by any means. Its reporters and editors, however, did take direct orders from Tory politics, and Sir John, up to his old tricks, made the paper aware of the date of the 1891 election while withholding the information from his rivals. By that time the *Mail* had abandoned the annexationist policies of Smith and had returned to a position of fierce if somewhat dotty independence in matters of concern to the caucus.

So unswerving was the *Empire* in its advance of Macdonald's interest that it lapsed into little less than melodramatic hysterics when its patron took ill in 1891. 'HE IS DYING!' exclaimed the *Empire* headline on May 30. 'A Great Career Nearing/ Its Close.' Various sub-heads, or decks, followed, each adding a bit more detail and despair. The prognosis was correct and Canada was indeed about to lose its greatest living figure, but the *Empire* behaved with the special lack of dignity reserved for distant relatives eager to emphasize their membership in the family. In abbreviated form, the headlines on successive days were:

SIR JOHN
The Premier is Still
Alive
BUT THAT IS ALL. (June 1)

LIFE EBBING.
The Premier's Great
Struggle.
ALL HOPE NOW GONE (June 2)

OUR PREMIER
He Still Holds Out
Against Death
BUT IS SINKING FAST
The Medical Bulletins Cause
Excitement
HOW LONG CAN HE LAST? (June 3)

HE STILL LIVES
Sir John's Vitality Is
Marvellous
'A RAY OF HOPE!' (June 4)

When the end came, on June 6, the paper printed heavy black rules between the columns and ran the headline:

HE IS REVERED.
Canada's Mourning for
the Premier.
THE SORROW OF TO-DAY.

The entire front page of June 12 was devoted to his funeral:

FAREWELL
The Dear Old Chief
at Rest.

With the dear old chief at rest, however, the paper that was his personal mouthpiece served little purpose to his successors, and Sir Mackenzie Bowell killed it off by selling it to the *Mail*, which thus in 1895 became the *Mail and Empire*.

Such polarization obtained everywhere, with journalists jockeying for patronage and preferments, which politicians doled out to them like the Devil granting Faust his wishes. Seeing how venal the system was, and how the loftiest motives were ascribed to such baseness, it is easy to sympathize with the frustration of those figures who stood aloof from it, and to know, for instance, what Carlyle must have meant when he blamed the 'idle population of editors' for England's involvement in the Crimean War. Yet such was the press of that time, and without it democracy, it was thought, could not function. Grattan O'Leary (1888-1976), who entered journalism by means of the Saint John *Standard*, another paper actually owned outright by the Conservative party, became the editor of the Ottawa *Journal* and at length was appointed to the Senate; as late as 1970, in his memoirs, he would argue that 'Strong editorial comment is inseparable from party affiliation. Unless it is a party press, it will not be a great press.' He was the last person in Canada known to have maintained such a stance. But the view was in a way merely the logical extension of the hardier one 'that there is no existing or historical example of a state without a functioning party not either governed by a dictatorship or undergoing revolution or civil war', as Harold A. Wills wrote in the Cochrane *Northland Post* in 1959, in an editorial typical of press pronouncements on the subject and Canadian opinion in general.

Some of the publications that made up the party press were disguised as religious ones, especially the ultramontane papers of Quebec, which advocated church rule or some system very close to it. Others were ostensibly ethnic papers, starting with *Teachdaire Gaidhealach Thasmania* (the first Gaelic paper in the New World, begun at Antigonish in 1837) and carrying on later in the century with Yiddish, German, Polish, Hungarian, Ukrainian, Swedish, and even Icelandic papers in splendid array, particularly in Toronto and Winnipeg. One of special interest is the *Canadian Jewish Times*, the nation's first English-language Jewish publication, begun in 1897 by the civil-libertarian journalist William T.C. Ryan (1839-1910). Still other newspapers were addressed to a certain economic class, as with the workingmen's press, which for a time might said to have included the Toronto *News*, in the days when Phillips Thompson (1843-1933) helped make it a voice

THE CHANGING LOOK OF NEWSPAPERS. Advances in technology, as regards paper manufacture as well as typesetting and press work, resulted in the gradual change in the size and design of Canadian newspapers. The *Niagara Spectator* of 1818 (figure 1) was the typical colonial publication, small in its dimensions and strictly vertical in its layout, with proclamations, adverts, and essays intermingled on its front page. By the end of the nineteenth century, newspaper pages were bigger and had more columns; but the type was relieved by line drawings and cartoons, and the stories were codified through a complex system of headline styles—as exemplified in the *Sunday World* and *Evening News* of Toronto, 1895 (2 & 3). The same approach still obtained on the day in 1900 when the Brantford *Expositor* (4) reported a turning-point in the South African War. For its part, the Edmonton *Evening Journal*, in announcing provincial status for Alberta in 1905 (5), contained the exciting news above the fold, reserving the rest of page one for advertising. Later that same year, however, the innovative *Toronto World* (6) was making the most of the still-new process for reproducing halftone photographs. Figure 7 shows an issue of the *Hamilton Spectator* from 1931 when photos had lost their novelty and grown smaller but were being used to break up a welter of stories both trivial and important. Such a busy look persisted in most urban centres until the 1960s.

THE NIAGARA SPECTATOR.

PRINTED AND PUBLISHED FOR AMOS McKENNE[illegible], IN THE TOWN OF NIAGARA, (U. C.)
(Next door South of Alex'r Rogers' Hotel.)

VOL. II.] THURSDAY, JULY 9, 1818. [NO. 19.

CONDITIONS.
THE
NIAGARA SPECTATOR

Will be published every Thursday, at [illegible] Dollars per annum.

All Subscriptions for less than a year, [illegible] by mail, must be paid in advance.

ADVERTISEMENTS

Not exceeding a square, will be conspicuously inserted once for a Dollar—and [illegible] shillings for every subsequent insertion. No single insertion will be considered less than a square.

No Advertisement will be discontinued without orders, and all arrearages paid.

All letters and communications must be post paid.

PRINTING
BLANKS, CARDS, HAND-BILLS,
&c. &c. &c.
EXECUTED WITH NEATNESS AND EXPEDITION.

By His Excellency Sir John Coape Sherbrooke, Knight Grand Cross of the most Honorable Military order of the Bath, Commander of His Majesty's Forces in the Provinces of North America.

A PROCLAMATION.

WHEREAS, heretofore for the purposes of maintaining the means of Circulation, and answering the exingencies of the Public service, His Excellency Sir George Provost Baronet, then Commanding His Majesty's Forces in British N. America, did make and prepare a number of Bills denominated Army Bills, and caused the same from time to time to be issued from the Army Bill Office, established for that purpose at the [illegible] the Provisions of the several Acts of the Province of Lower-Canada, made for the purpose of facilitating the Circulation of of Army Bills: and, whereas it is fit & proper that the Accounts of the said Army Bill Office should be closed; I have therefore thought fit to issue this Proclamation, hereby requiring all Persons holding Army Bills, to present the same for Payment at the Army Bill Office, in the City of Quebec, on or before the thirty-first day of October next, on which day the Army Bill Office will be finally closed: And in default of such presentation for Payment within that period, the holders of such Army Bills cannot receive or claim from the Military Chest the Payment thereof.

Given under my Hand & Seal at Arms at the Castle of Saint Lewis in the City of Quebec, the 1st day of May, in the year of our Lord one thousand eight hundred and eighteen, in the fifty-eight year of His Majesty's Reign.

(Signed)
J. C. SHERBROOKE.
By His Excellency's Command.
(Signed)
T. F. ADDISON,
Military Secretary. 20w 13

FOR SALE,
AT THIS OFFICE,
THE
CHURCH CATECHISM.
By the Gross, Dozen, or Single.

FROM THE KINGSTON GAZETTE.

MR. GOURLAY,
To the worthy Inhabitants of the District of Niagara.
(CONTINUED.)

Prescott is situated at one corner of the township of Augusta, where dwell Solomon Jones, J. C. D. John Bethune, Clerk, H. Walker, D. C. and others of notoriety. Arrangements being made in this township for the meeting of which I have given account in the Kingston Gazette of 2d. inst. I made an excursion through Oxford, Wolford, Kitley, Elmsly, Bastard, Yonge and Elizabethtown; in all of which townships I found the people greatly pleased with our proposals.

By holding a meeting in Augusta, every [illegible] that I could have no view towards *lowering* the character of those who had wantonly attacked mine. The character of these people was quite low enough; they had brought themselves into a dilemma, from which nothing but candid confession and apology could extricate them; and, as I had heard at Kingston, that there were, among them, some who regretted what they had done, my design was, after establishing a few facts, before the collective body of their neighbours, to afford an opportunity for reconciliation, by declaring myself willing to forgive every one who should confess his error. Unfortunately a very different spirit than that of repentance prevailed in the breasts of these infatuated men. I was no sooner arrived at the place of meeting, than, apprized of a combination among them to outstare the truth, and, that this combination was strengthened by partizans from other townships. I had not, prior to my arrival in Augusta, been acquainted with a single individual of that township, who attended this meeting, yet many came forward and shook hands with me most cordially, and one gentleman handed me a note intimating, that, five to one, were in my favour.

'Knowing the confusion which a combination, even of a few desperate characters, can produce in a multitude, I called for, and obtained, a list of those present [illegible] against the interference of others, and required that every fact, established before the meeting, should be committed, immediately, to writing. A Clerk was, for these purposes, nominated by the meeting, and was paid for his trouble, by some of the gentlemen present, who were desirous of regular proceedings.

In my published account of this meeting, I waved a recital of the disgusting conduct of the band of desperadoes, and am sorry to think, that, in His Majesty's dominions, I should witness such indecency: certainly, at home, I never had experience of such a spirit of insolent hardihood. What was asserted by one, was denied by another of the gang—what was recorded openly as the sense of the meeting was contradicted as soon as its bearing against the culprits was discovered; but, perhaps the tissue of palpable falsehoods published by them, without a name in the Kingston Gazette of the 9th June, forms the best evidence, taken in connection with the idiotcy of holding a second meeting, to console themselves with *victory*, after I was—*eighty miles off!!*

The name of Mr. Jonas Jones should not have been mentioned by me, had his associates not announced him. Till the 27th May, I had been given to believe that he possessed some share of sense and discretion. Alas! what can we think of a Member of Parliament who espouses such a cause as that of the so-called Committee of Augusta? It was Mr. Jones who was haranguing against our Address to the Regent, when I and the major part of the people left the meeting, disgusted with an intruder persisting in declaiming on a subject wholly foreign to the business at issue: indeed, at any rate, the Address of the District of Niagara, ought not to have been a subject of *complaint*. It was printed merely to give the public an opportunity of improving upon it, by *dispassionate* criticism; and, every District has a right to present such an Address as best suits the ideas or need of its inhabitants. The Inhabitants of Niagara, by no means, wished to press their's upon any one. If the friends of Mr. Jones—the Judge, the Priest and the Scribe, think that all is over, they may yet be mistaken. We may have to submit to the slang of common vagabonds; but there are ways of making men in office *feel* for their misconduct; and, I trust, that neither the Governor, nor Bishop of Canada, will prove insensate to the gross violation of decency and common sense, in a District Judge, or, established Clergyman.

The following is a copy of the notes taken at the meeting; and attested by the Clerk's signature.

At a meeting of Inhabitants of the township of Augusta, held at the house of Isaac Hurd, the 27th May, 1818—Richard Arnold, Esq. in the chair; it was moved and carried unanimously, that the names of the persons present be recorded.

2d. Mr. Gourlay having invited only "the Inhabitants of Augusta" to meet him at Isaac Hurd's, enters his protest against all those who [illegible] *resident inhabitants*, speaking or [illegible] on this occasion.

3d. In the newspaper containing Resolutions of "the Committee of the Inhabitants of Augusta," Oliver Lucet, misprinted for Oliver [illegible].

4th. The meeting [illegible] the Committee was appo[illegible] regular, annual and legal [illegible] meeting.

5th. Heman Landen, E[illegible] was at the meeting which appointed the Committee, and, says, 'he thinks [illegible] Simpson was not appointed.'

(Signed) JOHN PENNOCK, Clerk.

On the 28th May I reached Johnstown, and next day proceeded by the stage, to the ferry house in Lancaster, leaving the pamphlets and papers at the stores and taverns, along the whole route. The 30th and 31st I passed through a considerable portion of Glengary, and, on the 1st June, got into the District of Ottaway, where I had most hearty welcome from the principal inhabitants. Mr. McDonell the present Member of Assembly for that District, Mr. Mears, the former member, Colonel Fortune, Mr. Grant, and many others, declared all equally willing to espouse the great public cause; and, assured me, that, though, on account of the extreme distance to York, they might not send a member to the convention, they would nevertheless approve of our measure for enquiry into the state of the Province, and advance a sum of money, in aid, proportionate to the contribution of any other District.

On the 3d June I retraced my steps into the upper part of Glengary, and had the pleasure to find the people already alive in our country's interest. It had been, with much [illegible], that I could [illegible] now, they were cheerfully [illegible]; and, through the zeal of one worthy individual, I was able to attend two training meetings on the 4th of June. At the first I discovered that some ignorant individuals had been prejudiced against the cause; at the second, in Williamstown, open war had been declared against it by leading characters; but at both places I had the satisfaction to see how easy it was, by explanation, to give a very different cast to the countenances around me; and at both places, I left many sincerely willing to exert themselves, in forwarding our views.

Kingston, 29th June, 1818.

On my approach to Cornwall on the 5th June, I had intimation of strange proceedings which had gone on there, and in the neighbourhood, the day preceding—the burning of pamphlets and papers, and threatened burning of me in effigy. My stay in the village was short, but both here and onward, quite sufficient to afford me abundant information, as there were persons every where anxious to speak out their disgust of words and actions which had shocked their feelings and cast a stain on the character of the country.

When a single individual, moved by sudden passion, commits an act of madness, or gives vent to indecent language, our pity looks wistfully to the effect of some returning sense of shame, and we trust that conscience, alone, will soon carry her point. When a number of men conspire together for wicked purposes—act in concert—have the hardihood to publish their sentiments and proceedings—by mutual support suppress the influences of conscience and by noisy triumph carry along with them the thoughtless multitude, then, active measures are called for in opposition,—then, it is improper to set bounds to the severity of judgment, or, to restrain any expression which can paint iniquity in appropriate colours;—then we must no longer be softened by pity towards the guilty, but alarm society against the dangerous inroads of hardened vice and immorality.

The speech which was read to the training meeting in Stormont and elsewhere, now published in the Montreal Herald, and which I have desired to be inserted in the Niagara Spectator, infamous as it is, gives but a faint idea of the filthy sentiments of its promulgators, or of their worse than filthy acts. The profanity of Chrysler, the Member of Assembly, with the gross and blackguard conduct and designs of several of the friends and pupils of Dr. Strachan, can only be believed, when proved with all the solemnity of a court of justice, and to this the subject is now likely to be brought. The process may give much personal trouble to me; but the country will receive benefit by the agitation of such questions, and the full developement of truth.

All the way up to Brockville, which I reached by the 9th June, more and more information was afforded me, and the fullest conviction took hold of my mind, that even to that place, a correspondence and sympathy had existed among our enemies. So early as the 29th May, on which day I departed from Johnstown downwards, by the stage, active operations against our views had been commenced by the enemy; one of whom had followed close [illegible] in a little one horse waggon and pulled down our advertisements put up at the taverns, [illegible] the [illegible] with which they were stuck up was dry.

Passion proceeds from various points and from various unhallowed feelings and desires, has tended to strengthen outrage; and at no point—from no worthy feeling or desire can a rational pretext for the actors or their aiders and abettors be found. From the commencement of my writing on public topics in Canada, I have never been the first to offend; nay, it is well known to you for three months after my first essay, while I had not yet named a single individual resident in this Province with disrespect, I bore all sorts of personal abuse without designing to reply. When I did find it necessary to go into action against public men and measures I struck hard, not in anger but in duty; and, for the [illegible] truth alone. At this moment I am [illegible] perfectly convinced that nothing less could have answered the purpose. There was a species of morbid decay and corruption fast rooted in this Province, which mild treatment could not reach; and, without harshness there was no possibility of putting down the clamour of fools. My spirit is the very opposite of what many little minded people have imagined. I am a lover of peace and retirement—an admirer of all that nature places before us to lead on to harmony and good order. In my boyhood my chief delight was found among the flowers of the [illegible] of warm hearted companions. Alas! how glad should I be, did the stern duties of manhood yet suffer me to indulge myself with these!

On my present journey I have not been acting for myself. I undertook the business for the Niagara Committee and what I undertake I shall never trifle with. I have circulated the pamphlets and papers entrusted to my care below Lake Ontario, as other four persons sent to the Western, London, Gore, the Midland and Newcastle Districts have been charged to do. Not a particle of responsibility for what is contained in these publications attaches to me more than to thousands besides, who have adopted their principles and given them circulation; but in Brockville—in Augusta—in Cornwall, and elsewhere, personal pique, ignorance, contumacy and revenge have stirred up a host against me. In the publications of Niagara District, all is open, frank, liberal and plain, yet malignant and uncharitable spirits, out of their own evil imaginations have conjured up, out of these publications, mean insinuations and the basest accusations of secrecy—of hypocracy—of every odious intention and desire; because these grovelling wretches never soared into the regions of benevolence;—because they cannot see truth through the midst of their own iniquity; because they cannot think it possible that any one, for the sake of virtue and the general advancement of human happiness, can bestow his time, his labour, and his utmost desire—therefore they will rage in anger and drag us down to their hellish abodes.

On the 11th of June I returned to Kingston; and here occurred the most important event of my journey—an occurrence demanding the most serious attention of every man of Upper Canada, who boasts of independence. Sitting after dinner with some friends at our wine the day of my arrival here, I was called out & arrested by a warrant signed by T. Markland J. P. Always obedient to law, I immediately waited on the Magistrate and was told by him that he had issued the Warrant *by the authority and under the direction of the Attorney General, through the agency of Mr. Hagerman, and on the oath of Mr. Miles the Printer.* With this declaration, and bail to the amount of one thousand pounds being required and given, the affair waits for issue at the next Kingston Assizes: the issue will declare the fate of this country for years to come—if it is to labor under the Administration of fools, or quickly rise, by its own manly spirit, to that dignity which the finest Province, under British dominion ought to maintain.

To me this occurrence is most serious. It deranges all my plans of returning to my family and management of my private affairs; but I submit with the utmost cheerfulness in the full hope that whatever misfortune it may bring upon me, as an individual, it will eventually forward the great cause in which we are embarked. That the libel with which I am charged as the publisher is contained in the Address of His Royal Highness the Prince Regent I have no doubt, and I may call to mind how openly—how deliberately—how dispassionately that address was considered when in manuscript, before the fifteen Representatives of the Townships of Niagara District assembled at St. Catharine's, the [illegible] May last; and [illegible] with [illegible] of attention and care it was scanned over, sentence after sentence, by the Committee, next day, both in my presence and when I was required to withdraw, that the Committee might thereby be free from delicacy in making their remarks and amendments. In short, if ever any production was that of a body of men calmly met to consider of their constitutional rights and act upon them in honesty and pure intentions, this Address is one; and as such it must be defended. I composed it to express as nearly as possible the present feeling of the people of Upper Canada, and were I to compose it again I would not mince its declarations, for they are true. In defending them I shall assume high grounds. We are entitled to do so, and to descend one step, will be giving up all—No my worthy friends, not an inch of the ground we stand upon must be given up, for, give up that inch and a new series of years of humility and degradation must mark the history of Upper Canada. For once let us by firm conduct, maintain the law—fly in the face of arbitrary power—mark, with due reprobation, the neglects of ministers, and then we may expect to enjoy not only peace but prosperity,—then we shall no longer have need to appeal to our Sovereign for redress; rulers will respect the laws, and, well administered laws, will insure respect from the [illegible]

Some of the best informed people of this place have told me that they think Hagerman, the agent in this business, capable of taking upon him to order the arrest without any positive authority from the Attorney General. This Hagerman is brother of the petulant fellow who cut such a figure at Earnest Town, and of another who, I am told, was many years confined in the States prison for forgery, now reported to be hanged; but for all this I am of a different opinion.

When I wrote my second address to the resident Land Owners of Upper Canada in the beginning of February last, the Honorable William Dickson who was so well pleased with it as to offer me 500 acres of land, for the good it was likely to produce to the Province, said, that if the people in York would now but arrest me, the business would be completed. Unfortunately they did not then think it prudent, although to a certainty that Address contained matter as libellous as that for which I am now to be tried. In that case I had offered to prove the truth of what I asserted before the bar of Parliament. Truth proved before a Jury of independent men, I trust, will render our assertions equally safe. It has been said the greater the truth the greater the libel; but there is a mighty odds between truth wantonly told to the injury of an individual, and those great truths which must be told to support the dignity of a misgoverned people, and as a protest against insulted laws—truth told by one and truth told by thousands—truth bursting from the honorable feelings of a loyal people—truth which ought not and cannot be concealed.

When the Hon. William Dickson returned from the Parliamentary session at York, and had ceased to be my friend, then I heard he was anxious to have me arrested from different motives from those which two months before had occurred to him—then, I heard, he entreated Colonel Claus to arrest me for my address of the 2d April; but Col. Claus, it was said, very prudently declined, telling Mr. D. he might as well do it himself.

Mr. D. crossed with me in the Steam-Boat to York; and it does seem possible that, upon the additional ground of the address to the Prince Regent, then just published, he may have prevailed with the Attorney General, who was the apprentice of his apprentice—it is grandson in legal erudition—to assume a power detested by every good man at home—that of proceeding by an *ex-officio* process.

1

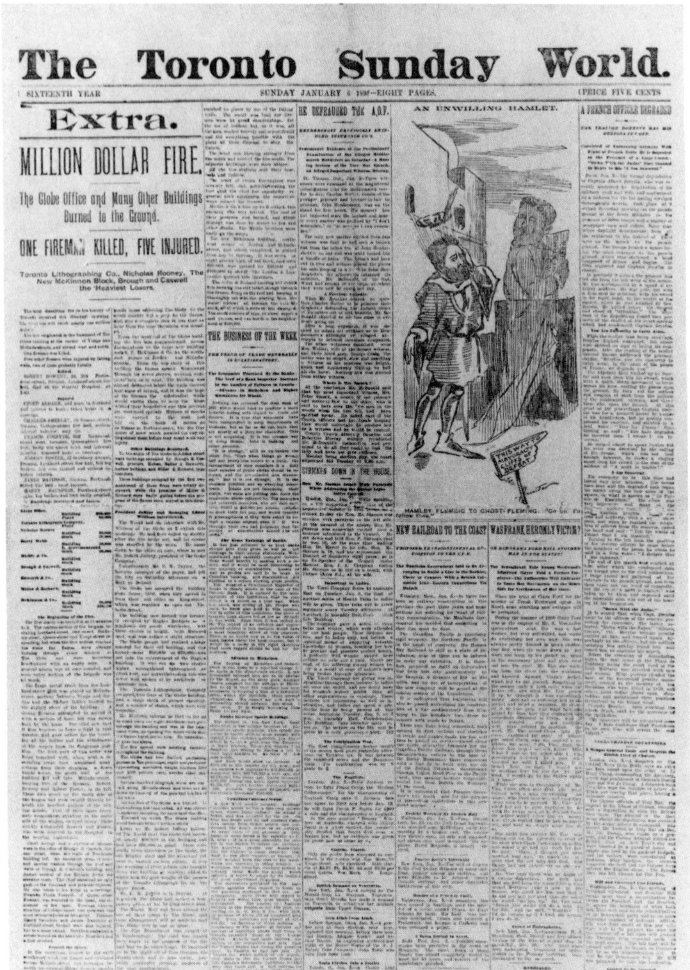

The Toronto Sunday World.

SIXTEENTH YEAR — SUNDAY JANUARY 6 189[illegible]—EIGHT PAGES. — PRICE FIVE CENTS

Extra.

MILLION DOLLAR FIRE.

The Globe Office and Many Other Buildings Burned to the Ground.

ONE FIREMAN KILLED, FIVE INJURED.

Toronto Lithographing Co., Nicholas Rooney, The New McKinnon Block, Brough and Caswell the Heaviest Losers.

THE BUSINESS OF THE WEEK

HE DEFRAUDED THE A.O.F.

STRICKEN DOWN IN THE HOUSE.

AN UNWILLING HAMLET.

HAMLET FLEMING TO GHOST-FLEMING. "Go on. I'll follow thee."

NEW RAILROAD TO THE COAST

WAS FRANK HER ONLY VICTIM?

A FRENCH OFFICER DEGRADED

2

EXTRA THE EVENING NEWS. EDITION

THE GREATEST CIRCULATION IN CANADA.

VOLUME XIV. NO. 248. TORONTO, MONDAY MARCH 4, 1895 PRICE ONE CENT.

ABOUT $1,000,000

Toronto Visited by a Third Disastrous Fire Within Two Months.

SIMPSON'S BLOCK GONE.

A Dozen Other Places of Business at Yonge and Queen Streets Suffer Great Damage.

PERHAPS THE WORK OF FIRE BUGS.

The Only Way of Accounting for the Disaster —Robert Simpson's Loss Well on to Half a Million—He Will Rebuild—Jamieson's and Sutcliffe's Establishments Completely Wrecked —The Tremont House Gutted—Knox Church Steeple Gone.

THE SIMPSON BLOCK BEFORE THE FIRE.

THE SCENE OF THE CONFLAGRATION.

THE RUINS OF THE SIMPSON BLOCK.

3

ALWAYS WEAR Dempster HATS

THE EXPOSITOR.

ALWAYS WEAR Dempster HATS

VOL. XXVIII.—Whole Number 8145. BRANTFORD, ONTARIO, SATURDAY, MAY 19, 1900. $3.00 PER ANNUM

A Perfect Watch

ALEX. MOFFAT,

WANTS.

TO RENT.

FOR SALE.

Mafeking Has Been Relieved

BRITISH ENTERED IN TRIUMPH

BOERS ADMIT THEY WERE FOILED

The Gallant Garrison Mafeking After Seven Months Siege

HAS BEEN RELIEVED

The Cry of "Pass the Loaf" Has Been Heard and Answered.

STRONG MOUNTED FORCE

Sent up by Roberts.. Forced Its Way in.

Boers Admit They Have Abandoned the Siege For Good.

GREAT REJOICING

The Whole Empire Rings With the Praises of the Men

WHO DEFIED THE

Boers Amid Shot, Shell, Fever and Starvation.

COL. BADEN-POWELL, COMMANDER OF THE BRITISH FORCES AT MAFEKING

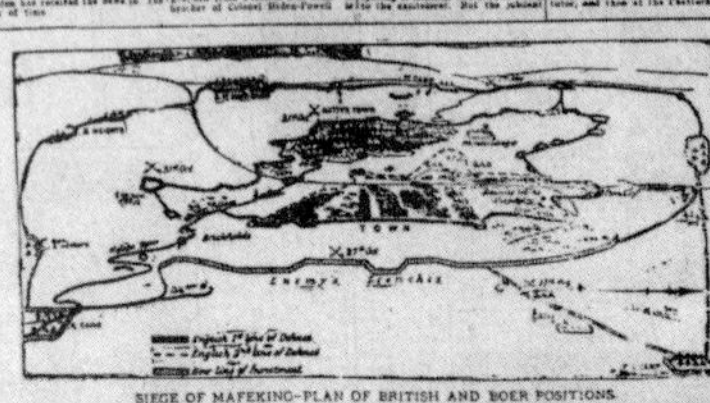

SIEGE OF MAFEKING—PLAN OF BRITISH AND BOER POSITIONS

Trouserings

A fine assortment of bright new trouserings for the season. $4.00, 5.00, 5.50, 6.00.

THOMSON, The Tailor,

WANT MONEY

Y.M.C.A. Directors Resolves Upon an Important Move.

EXCURSION TO NIAGARA.

THE EVENING JOURNAL

VOL. 2, No 249. EDMONTON, ALBERTA, SATURDAY, SEPTEMBER 2, 1905. PRICE FIVE CENTS.

Alberta, a Province.

HISTORY IN THE MAKING IN ALBERTA'S NEW CAPITAL.

Inauguration of the Province Marked by Fine Weather, a Big Crowd, an Impressive Ceremony, Games, and Military Review.

Addresses by the Governor-General, Premier Laurier, the Lieutenant-Governor, Honorable Wm. Paterson, Sir Gilbert Parker, and Mayor MacKenzie.

A. C. Rutherford, Premier of Alberta.

LIEUT-GOVERNOR REPLIES.

THE INAUGURAL BALL.

BALL FOR ALBERTA.

BECOMING A NATION.

VICTORIAN IGNORED.

INSURANCE FRAUDS.

A PATRIOTIC ADDRESS.

ILLUSTRATED SECTION

The Toronto World.

NEW ONTARIO NUMBER

PART I—PAGES 1 TO 8 | TORONTO, ONT., SUNDAY, NOVEMBER 26, 1905 | PRICE FIVE CENTS

Northern New Ontario---The Canadian Settlers' Land of Promise

ON THE WHITE RIVER, FOURTEEN MILES NORTH OF NEW LISKEARD—STEAMER BOUND FOR TOWNTOWN.

Nowhere Else on the America Continent are Greater Advantages Offered.

A Country That Literally Flows With Milk and Honey and All the Other Good Things.

Water-Power and Pulp Wood

Prominent Citizens of New Ontario

S. H. LENNON | J. A. McKELVEY | J. A. OSBORNE

FOUNTAIN FALLS ON THE MONTREAL RIVER, NEW ONTARIO

A "PEBBLE" FROM THE TIMMINS MINE, NEW ONTARIO

TORONTO UNIVERSITY FOOTBALL TEAM, INTERCOLLEGIATE CHAMPIONS OF 190

HOME EDITION
28 PAGES

The Hamilton Spectator

THE WEATHER
Fair and Cool

HAMILTON CANADA SATURDAY MAY 23 1931 — PRICE TWO CENTS

Germany Defeated — Demand For Statement of Armaments From World Powers By Berlin Is Refused—Page 1

Sporting News on Page 22

Storms Predicted — Shipping On Lower Lakes Warned of Severe Northwest Gales Over Week-End—Page 1

Markets Stocks Page 26

Seek Lower Rates — Applications For Decreases in Freight Charges Predicted in United States—Page 6

DECLINE IN SILVER HARMS WORLD TRADE

Eastern Nations' Buying Power Destroyed

Causes of Drop in Prices Are Analyzed

HIGH HONOR

RT. HON. ARTHUR HENDERSON

British foreign minister, who has been elected chairman of the forthcoming disarmament conference.

SWEEPSTAKES SCHEME GROWS TO VAST SIZE

Started With Two Men in Bare Room As Office

Seven Million Wagered on Epsom Derby

Money Pours in From All Over World

AS SPANISH MOBS BROKE LOOSE

DEMANDS MADE BY THE SOVIET ARE DISPUTED

Quota Sought in Wheat Exports Unreasonable

Canada and U. S. Occupy the Premier Place

Russia Had Dropped Out of the Markets

WHEAT CONFERENCE COMES TO A CLOSE

GAVE HIS LIFE

BRIGADIER-GENERAL R. H. DUNLAP

Ferguson Asserts Parley Has Been Success

Advisory Body is Created At Last Session

SPORT RUINED BY SWEEPSTAKE CRAZE ABROAD

Interest in Great Derby Has Been Diverted

Wild Orgy of "Something For Nothing"

Old Country Suffers From Rainy Week-Ends

UNITY OF CAPITAL AND LABOR SOUGHT

Both Forces Urged To Co-operate By Vatican

Full Text of the Encyclical Now Released

MANUFACTURERS WILL ASSEMBLE

Sixtieth Anniversary of C.M.A. Observed

Delegates Are Gathering At Victoria

BRIAND GIVEN GREAT OVATION ON HIS RETURN

People Stormed Station To Do Him Honor

Likely To Reconsider His Resignation

Women Give Minister Strong Support

GRANDSON OF PRESIDENT IS FATALLY SHOT

Garfield Found Dead in Room At His Home

Believed To Have Taken His Own Life

Had Distinguished Career As Soldier

GERMANS MEET WITH DEFEAT

Nations Refuse To Divulge Armament Power

Berlin Sought Statement From Powers

POSTAL REVENUE SHOWS DEFICIT

Hoover To Examine Huge Expenditures

Predecessors Regarded It As Public Service

CARDINAL ON WAY TO ROME

Segura Leaves Spain After Recent Letter

May Become Member of Congregation of Rites

DESERTED SHIP DRIVEN ASHORE

Two-Masted Fishing Vessel Wrecked On Coast

Crew Escaped Before the Disaster

PACIFISTS TO LODGE PROTEST

Will Demonstrate During Aerial Maneuvers

Object To Warlike Display At New York

STORMS LIKELY ON LOWER LAKES

Warnings Are Displayed At Cleveland To-day

Strong Northwest Winds To Sweep Waters

RIOTING OCCURS AMONG WORKLESS

Serious Clashes in Central German Cities

Barricades On Streets Erected At Essen

INDEPENDENCE

Unionist Party of Porto Rico Launches Campaign

GRIM TRAGEDY

BRIEF CLASH

NATIONAL RIGHTS

FREE TO DEPART

NEW DESTROYER

POLAND REBUFFED

HYDROPLANE TESTED

RIVER IN FLOOD

CANCELS C.N.R. TRAIN

7

of the Knights of Labour. But another fact complicated the pattern: the fact that mainstream journalists played politics at the municipal and provincial levels as well as at the federal—indeed, played politics quite as much as the politicians themselves, motivated by the same unstable mixture of power and public service. Perhaps it is well to consider some examples from various periods and various cities.

That editors should involve themselves in local politics seems natural, inevitable, and generally desirable, given the intensely local character of daily newspapers throughout most of the nineteenth century. The local editor, particularly one who was his own proprietor, was after all a businessman and perhaps better educated than most, with a more fully realized sense of community and also, if he were successful enough, an instinct for *noblesse oblige*. The tendency to see the editor in a political role had its basis in the colonial period, when persons of learning and relative achievement were so few that most had to fill any number of useful roles. Their example continued to be followed on the Prairies relatively late in the day, as frontier conditions were replicated there in one new settlement after another, even into the twentieth century. But there is a subtle though crucial difference between some village editor and power-broker on the one hand and, for example, Brown Chamberlin (1827-97) on the other. Chamberlin was a barrister (always a promise of villainy there!) who was the proprietor of the Montreal *Gazette* between 1853 and 1867, when he won a seat in the Confederation parliament. He resigned his seat in 1870 to become Queens' Printer, a post that continued to be a rich patronage plum many decades after the United States, by comparison, abolished the equivalent job, setting up the Government Printing Office in 1860 as part of the civil service.

Conflict of interest as such, a concept that journalists might run afoul of in playing politics, is a relatively modern notion, and it is only with the arrogance of the living that one can use it to condemn the dead. But one can at least trace its coming. There were indeed a few eyebrows raised, if only in resignation, when, in the 1930s, a man with the wonderful name Bert Wemp (1889-

1976) served simultaneously as mayor of Toronto and city editor of the *Telegram*, a newspaper that was accustomed to proposing, and usually helping to elect, its own slate of aldermen and controllers but until then had stopped short of running its own employees. Yet that case was not really so different from most, in which political posts were given out as rewards for journalistic usefulness.

In instances where the office preceded the position in journalism, there was not the same question of impropriety: Henri Bourassa, the strident French-Canadian nationalist leader (1875-1952), was the mayor of Montebello, Quebec, before entering federal and then provincial politics and in 1910 founding *Le Devoir* as an amplifier for his views. But what about such cases as Dr Joseph-Charles Taché (1820-94), editor of *Le Courrier du Canada* and MLA for Rimouski, who then became a prison inspector (the prison board being one of the more notorious patronage sloughs in Victorian Ottawa)? Or Arthur Harvey (1834-1905), who became the Finance Department's statistician after a long career at the Hamilton *Spectator*, the Montreal *Gazette*, and the Quebec *Morning Telegraph*, true Tory papers all of them? Or William Gillespy (1824-86), the editor and proprietor of the Hamilton *Spectator*, who followed that significant achievement with a career as a customs official (another common reward for service by one of the lads)? The list could be made very long.

It is well to remember, however, that all of the jobs named seem relatively modest. The point of the gesture was to reward journalists and ensure their safe retirement, not to make them rich. Many proprietors, however, did become wealthy and in so doing engaged in politics at a much higher level than did parliamentary correspondents or even editors. The James Beaty who has been mentioned already as the proprietor of the Toronto *Leader*, and who at other times owned the *Patriot* and the *Colonist*, was a director of the Grand Trunk and used his publications to further his railway schemes. He later sat in the House of Commons. Hugh Graham, who seems never to have failed to consider the devious solution to whatever problem was at hand, used both the Montreal *Star*, which of course he owned, and *La Minerve*, on which he held a loan at the time, to endorse his own railway plans. Then in 1904 he secretly bought control of *La Presse* for $750,000 and used it for the same purpose, as well as to frustrate Laurier. As late as the Great War, Col. J.W. Stewart found that he needed ownership of the Vancouver *Sun* to fight for a railway franchise. His contemporary, W.F. (Billy) Maclean (1854-1919), discovered a similar latent utility in the Toronto *World*, which also advanced the insistent views of its editor, Albert Edward Stafford Smythe, on theosophy (which he favoured) and venereal disease (which he opposed).

This sometimes indistinct blend of journalism and politics was a vital part of Canada's political culture and, in an age when newspapers were the only source of news, was accepted by the citizenry without much serious thought, as part of the abiding pageant. Such was the intermingling of the press and politics that on election nights crowds would gather in the street outside newspaper offices with ears cocked and eyes peeled for early returns from the hustings (perhaps a type of behavioural residue from the days of public executions). They would, of course, join the throng at the newspaper of a particular party or faction, the one down the street being a deceitful rag that no person of sound mind would believe or even condone. Many publications posted daily bulletins in their front windows for the edification of passersby, even on ordinary days. As late as the Second World War the Vancouver *Sun* and its enemy, the *Province*, one block away, would compete for the attention of pedestrians with appropriate bulletins in huge black type, stuck up at intervals in the street-level windows.

At election time the intimate and intricate relationship between readers and newspapers was often heightened to an almost unnatural degree, illustrating clearly the climate in which the party press held sway. In 1886 Judge H.S. Cayley of the *Herald* in Calgary was given a torchlight parade to celebrate the fact that friends in Ottawa had succeeded in having him released from gaol, where he had been reposing as a result of a long political argument in print; the groundswell of support was enough to send him to the legislative council. During an election in 1897, the editor of the *Saskatchewan Herald* in Battleford got word that a mob was intending to raid the newsroom. A Mountie stayed up all night in the newspaper's office, reading the paper with all the lamps on, conspicuously visible from the street. That was enough to make the vigilantes think better of their plan. As late as 1911 patrons who had forgathered outside the offices of the *Mail and Empire* grew so excited at the election returns coming in that they proceeded to the respective buildings of the Toronto *Daily Star* and the *Globe*, two journals set apart by their Liberal direction, and broke the windows at both places. Neither mobs nor issues of national significance, however, were needed to stir political passion to the point of direct action.

In the 1890s, during Toronto's long controversy about whether streetcars should be operated on the Sabbath and if so by whom—a debate repeated in Ottawa and other cities—the moral and economic questions were overshadowed for a time by the doings of the press. The *Telegram* so ruthlessly attacked a pro-Sunday-streetcar alderman named Farquhar that he set upon the publisher, John Ross Robertson, with a whip. The two of them fell to wrestling in the street while a disinterested third party pelted them with eggs. The tussle ended with Farquhar retreating to the premises of the more sympathetic *News*. But Robertson followed him and lay in wait. When Farquhar at length emerged, Robertson pinned him to the ground and, in a form of torture, 'read one of my editorials to him'. Horsewhipping editors in an excess of democratic zeal was a remarkably common practice in the era of the party press; one of the last documented instances occurred in 1914 when an outraged female reader took rawhide to the back of the Ottawa *Journal*'s editor.

In squabbles amongst its own members, the party press was nowhere more fierce than in Montreal, though it is also true to say that nowhere else were the partisan divisions so clouded by sectarian concerns. And once certain English-language papers elsewhere, such as the *Star* and *Telegram* in Toronto, began to refocus their energies more along lines of class than of party dogma, certain French papers took up the idea with gusto. This was particularly the case with *La Presse*, which was distinguished in its early years not only by its luridness but by its self-appointed yet indisputable position as the workingman's friend. It was therefore startling when Henri Bourassa started *Le Devoir*. 'Laurier and the Liberals, Tupper and the Conservatives, still had their followings for political purposes', wrote Augustus Bridle, the Toronto journalist and critic. 'Bourassa only claimed the supreme right to speak as the leader of the French-Canadian race.' *Le Devoir* was certainly 'for' the generality of French Canadians and just as certainly pro-Catholic. But it had no aspirations to address people on the strict basis of class or religion or even party politics, except to the extent that Bourassa's own personal views where given exploitable terms in the Nationalist party that he founded; in editorial terms this meant that its distinguishing attitude was an anti-English stand in all matters large and small.

Bourassa was a reformed Liberal. He had entered the House in 1896 with Laurier but soon broke with him over the use of Canadian troops in the Boer War. His importance was much more profound than the financial success of his paper would indicate; as late as 1920 it sold only slightly more than 20,000 copies per day. He was perhaps the last orator-editor, in the manner of Mackenzie and McGee; like the former especially, he was a gifted damner and contrarian. Bridle spoke with the full weight of Anglo-Canadian opinion when he called Bourassa 'the greatest mischief-maker in the Empire'. Writing in 1916—that is, before Bourassa came out against conscription during the First World War—Bridle went on to say that the mere fact that Bourassa 'is a free citizen, and that *Le Devoir* continues to circulate, is proof that the French Canadian has more rights under the British flag than he ever could have had under any flag of France'—a statement that says at least as much about the politics of the English press.

The 1890s saw the rise of what was called independent journalism: that is, of large, even sometimes monolithic papers that were independent of the political parties themselves without necessarily being in the least non-partisan. Put another way, independent journalism marked the rise of the editor as a full-fledged player in the political game, instead of a politicians' tool.

Narrowly defined, a list of such new papers would run in order to size from the *Times* in Kingston through the *News* in London to the *Tribune* in Winnipeg. The difference was often less one of substance than of disposition, though structural comparisons are sometimes revealing as well. In Vancouver, both the *Province* and the *Sun* date from this era, but while the first was 'independent', the second actually had support of the Liberals written into its corporate charter from 1890 until the late 1950s. The rise of the independent journalists, whether entrepreneurs who made great fortunes or editors who piled up their rewards in Heaven, were most conspicuous in Toronto and Winnipeg, where political rivalries were most intricately tied to the battle for commercial supremacy, as stronger newspapers gobbled up the weak ones, to the point where only a handful remained to fight for control of the expanding and immensely wealthy markets.

The most obvious example is the Toronto *Daily Star*. It began as the *Evening Star* in 1892 and was the strike sheet of local printers who had been locked out of the *News*, which clearly had abandoned its much-vaunted sympathy for the labouring class. The first editor was E.E. Sheppard from the *News*, but his role is not often remembered. Rather it is Joseph E. Atkinson (1865-1948) who is usually considered the 'founder' for the way he took over the paper in 1899, nurtured it, and made it in time the biggest newspaper in the country and reputedly one of the most profitable in North America. Holy Joe, as he was known, owing to steadfast Methodist beliefs and righteous asceticism, was a prohibitionist always, a pacifist except in wartime when it mattered, a master of applied tinkering insofar as newspaper technology was concerned, and, most importantly, a Liberal—one, moreover, who was sometimes inclined in the direction of socialism. This made for lively doings in the *Daily Star*'s war with the city's other one-cent evening paper, the *Telegram* of John Ross Robertson, which printed the Union Jack atop the front page every day and espoused views more or less indistinguishable from those of the Orange Lodge, the Conservative Party, and the chartered banks.

Atkinson's chief lieutenant, son-in-law, and eventual successor was Harry C. Hindmarsh (1887-1955), a bald, thick-set man with wire spectacles, silver dental work, and no discernible neck (when he smiled, which was seldom, he looked like a pipe wrench). He had come to prominence early in the new century by the vivid gruesomeness with which he had described a hanging, and was the *Star*'s city editor by 1915; he is said, typically but erroneously, to have fired the entire reporting staff one Christmas Eve. In fact his mark was that he contributed to Canadian journalism the notion of applying melodramatic, Hearstian techniques to left-wing ends. A flying squad of as many as forty reporters and photographers would descend on a single story like wolves and pick its bones of the last bit of sensationalist flesh. The *Star* was utterly irresponsible but irresistibly entertaining in the more than half-century during which it fought the *Telegram* for circulation and advertising.

Star men constantly seemed to be rescuing lost aviators in the North whether they wished to be rescued or not. Escaped criminals were forever surrendering to them and making the *Star* a gift of their life stories, which, like Atkinson's injections of Christian piety and Fabian philosophy, were supposed to work wonders on the young. If, in order to beat the *Telegram* at these games, a reporter had to break into the next-of-kin's home to purloin documents or disguise 'sob sisters' as parlourmaids, then so much the better. Whenever the *Telegram*, whose efforts were managed by colourful characters like John R. (Black Jack) Robinson (1862-1928) and the naval historical C.H.J. Snider (1879-1971), deigned to mention the *Star* at all, it referred to it as the *Red Star* or the *Toronto Daily Pravda*. Each paper won as many days as it lost, and the contest waxed and waned for years but was never entirely abandoned: too much depended on the outcome. Both institutions were so popular that they acquired power within their respective parties. Such was particularly the case as regards the *Star*, because Atkinson's height coincided with long periods of Liberal rule in Ottawa. His was definitely a case of the journalist as equal, as a contributor to policy and a public critic of it, rather than as a loyal servant. Only John W. Dafoe of the Winnipeg *Free Press* could exert such influence and he did so rather differently, being the editor, not the proprietor, of a paper that had loftier aspirations editorially. The *Star* was also therefore a very different voice of Liberal authority from the *Globe* as well.

On George Brown's death in 1880, the *Globe* was taken over by John Gordon Brown (1827-96), who had been his brother's trusted second-in-command. He served only briefly, and the paper passed into the hands of a business family, the Jaffrays, who in 1890 installed John (later Sir John) Willison (1856-1927) as editor. He was an astute political commentator and the Canada correspondent of *The Times* of London, and made himself the Canadian editor most respected for his knowledge of politics and statecraft before resigning in 1903 to pursue 'independent' journalism as the editor of what one of its veterans would call that 'university of culture, economics and general information known as the Toronto *News*'. The *News* had been bought for this purpose for only $150,000 by the businessman Joseph (in time, Sir Joseph) Flavelle. Senator Robert Jaffray then named the Rev. J.A. Macdonald (1862-1923), the former principal of a Presbyterian women's college, as editor of the *Globe*. One wag has explained how Macdonald 'became the editorial exponent of what was then regarded as the new Liberalism, which consisted in chastening the sins of the old Liberals. . . .' Others suspected him of being a propagandist for God or the caucus or both, but like Willison, he was not simply an imperialist in his sympathies but was anti-reciprocity as well and as such played some hand in helping to bring down Laurier in 1911, only to resign during the war when he was accused of being cool to the defence of Britain.

A similar situation existed in Winnipeg, with fierce competition among, at various times, three or four dailies, which together showed the evolving political function of the press in general. In the first nine years of the new century, Winnipeg's population went from 42,000 to 120,000 and by the Great War stood at fully 150,000. That such a booming market should attract new newspapers seems quite natural. The dominant participant in the field was the *Manitoba Free Press*, or so it became after its purchase in 1898 by the Hon. J.W. Sifton, who passed it in time to his son, the Liberal cabinet minister Sir Clifford Sifton (1861-1924), whose name would also be associated with the *Star*-

Phoenix in Saskatoon and the *Leader-Post* in Regina. It was with the Siftons that J.W. Dafoe (1866-1944) cast his lot, serving as editor of the *Free Press* for four decades and making it, as Frank Underhill observed in 1931 (the year it became the *Winnipeg Free Press*), 'the only newspaper in Canada which exercises anything approaching to a national influence'. As Heather Robertson has observed: 'It was no accident that Marshall McLuhan grew up reading the *Free Press*. The *Free Press* looked true.'

Its main adversary was the *Tribune*, established in 1890 by Robert Lorne Richardson, who had once been a journalist at the *Globe* in Toronto and then had come to Winnipeg and quarrelled with Dafoe. The first issue swore the usual oath to

> be an independent journal in the best sense of the word. By independence we do not mean neutrality. The public may expect to find this journal vigorously advocating all measures which it conceives to be in the interests of the Province of Manitoba and opposing just as strenuously all measures which it believes to be antagonistic to those interests.

In fact its politics were renegade Liberal, to the even greater annoyance of the *Free Press*, which would voice the party orthodoxy with increasing assurance through the years ahead and whose editors would even ghost-write the speeches of Liberal politicians. The other player was the Conservative *Telegram*, established in 1892. When Arthur Ford joined the *Telegram* in 1906, he found that

> There was not only a political feud in progress between the *Telegram* and the *Free Press* . . . but there was an intense rivalry between the staffs of the two papers. The day I joined the *Telegram* the city editor . . . took me into his private office and instilled into me that it was an ill-spent day that a *Telegram* reporter did not scoop the *Free Press*, and that it was perfectly legitimate to commit every deed, except murder, to accomplish this end.

Without being any less political than newspapers in the East, the press west of Winnipeg was generally less beholden to political parties, because of the newness of the cities and towns and also because party organization was not so strong there. Rather, the dailies in the three Prairie provinces were more inclined to embrace the fear of Ottawa over the fear of Washington in the reciprocity election of 1911. The conspicuous exception was the

Herald in Calgary, with its near-fanatical Toryism, but even the *Herald* nodded approvingly after quoting a candidate who said: 'Let a man be either a Liberal or Conservative, he must be a North West man first and for party afterwards.' A different political ethic existed in British Columbia, however.

The essentially British notion of the press baron, the proprietor who was a politician or statesman *ex officio*, moving easily in and out of public life, took hold in BC as nowhere else in Canada. John Robson (1824-92), followed swiftly on the heels of Amor De Cosmos both by becoming premier and by beginning a newspaper in 1860 first called the New Westminster *Times*, then the *British Columbian*, and finally the *Columbian*. Its next owner was James David Taylor, an MP and eventually a senator. There were few more wilfully Liberal papers than the Victoria *Times*, whose bonds to the Laurier government were virtually as strong as those of the Winnipeg *Free Press*; the trumpeting of the Liberals outlasted Laurier, through the editorship of B.C. (Benny) Nichols (1879-1936).

Vancouver, like Toronto, was a city in which the politicization began quite early, owing to a combination of market factors, the extreme intensity of the competition in particular, as well as to the presence of proprietors and editors who tended to be too eccentric to be contained within the old system of allegiance. The *Province* was founded in 1894 but was published in Victoria until it was bought by Walter C. Nichol (1866-1928), an emigré from the newsrooms of Ontario who became lieutenant-governor of BC. In its transplanted home it competed successfully against the *News-Advertiser*. M.E. Nichols recalled that in 1909 the *Province*'s 'building, the office, its furnishing, and the atmosphere were suggestive of a publisher deep in the problem of making ends meet.' But the impression was deceptive. At that time, Nichols claimed, it was one of only three or four Canadian papers with annual net earnings in excess of $100,000; by the 1930s, when Nichols himself was its publisher, the *Province* had become the first paper west of Toronto to attain a daily circulation of 100,000. It is also said that the *Province* was the only important daily in the country that did not mention a serious revolt in the

Conservative caucus in Ottawa, a story many other papers, Conservative as well as Liberal, displayed on their front pages. Nichols didn't believe in running down the party in public.

The cleverest operator, though, was his Liberal counterpart, R.J. Cromie (1887-1936), who bought the nearly bankrupt Liberal party organ, the *Morning Sun*, and later, in 1917, the *News-Advertiser* (which he put to death), and similarly the *World*, a PM. The vendor of the *World*, however, promptly re-entered the field with the *Evening Star* and carried on with it until 1926, when Cromie put together a remarkably imaginative deal in which the *Evening Star* bought the *Sun*'s circulation and switched to morning publication, while the morning *Sun* bought the *Star*'s circulation and became a PM, and the *World* was simply closed. There was one fewer paper than before, but the realignment heightened the competitiveness, and hence the potential profit, of those that remained. The *Star*, like the *News-Herald*, would pass away eventually, leaving the *Sun* and the *Province*. The political bickering, too, became more intense once the field was reduced.

In this, Vancouver was conforming to the nationwide pattern. Between 1914 and 1922 forty Canadian dailies ceased publication, swallowed up by rivals wishing more of the market for themselves. Such successful publishers on the grand scale might still have social philosophies in addition to the one that comes free with the accumulation of capital. Certainly they would continue to endorse candidates, platforms, and parties, and perhaps even to begrudge existence to those they did not support. They might even, like the owner of the Halifax *Chronicle* in the 1920s, consult with the provincial Liberal leaders on patronage appointments and other such matters, but they certainly no longer had need of political patronage, direct or indirect. The party press suffered a serious blow.

Another such challenge came with creation in 1917 of the Canadian Press co-operative wire service, at least insofar as it impacted on the Parliamentary Press Gallery.

In 1946, when David Legate of the Montreal *Star* was sent to the Press Gallery, he chanced to meet two politicians in the lift, and one of them, whom he knew, introduced him to the other.

'David has come up to cover the House for the *Star*,' said the one MP to the other, a member of the CCF, who replied, 'You mean, cover up the House for the *Star*.' For indeed that is what the job had long entailed.

The need for something like what is now the Press Gallery was apparent in the early days of responsible government. In 1850 the corps of partisan hacks who wrote puffs and libels about the Legislative Assembly and called themselves the press gallery, organized a boycott of the proceedings. Various similar groups followed, such as the Dominion Editors' and Reporters' Association founded in 1873, and special provision was made for such people in designs for the first Parliament Buildings in Ottawa. However, the institution in its present form dates to about 1880, though extant records go back no further than 1903. When Arthur Ford went to Ottawa on behalf of the Winnipeg *Telegram* early in the new century there were still members of the Press Gallery who went back to the 1880s. Then as now, however, it was a young person's game, and many illustrious careers were hatched there, including those of J.W. Dafoe, John Willison, and Joseph E. Atkinson. A list of other figures associated with the Press Gallery might include Ferdnand Rinfret, the editor of *Le Canada*; Georges Pelletier, the editor of *Le Devoir*; and P.D. Ross (1858-1949), the editor of the Ottawa *Journal*. Paul Bilkey (1878-1962), parliamentary correspondent for the Toronto *Mail and Empire* from 1912 to 1917, when he became editor of the Montreal *Gazette*, articulated that many correspondents felt when he described how membership in the Gallery gave one a view of the Commons that

> spoke eloquently of a mighty past. The entrance stones were worn by the feet of legislators, statesmen, and leaders who had lived their lives and died and whose names have become imperishable. In the green chamber, the desks and chairs were the same desks and chairs that Sir John Macdonald, Alexander Mackenzie, Edward Blake, the eloquent D'Arcy McGee, Cartier, Chapleau, Dorion, Langevin and all the others great and small had used since the first days of the Dominion.

Of course he was referring to the Parliament Buildings that were destroyed in the fire of 1916, an event that caused the annual Press

Gallery dinners to be abandoned for several years. In any case, because the Gallery was technically *of* as well as *in* Parliament, reporting to the Speaker of the House, it could not be raided by the RCMP in pursuit of liquor-law violators. In 1911 it had only 25 members, but they included representatives of *The Times* of London and several of the large American papers. Arthur Ford also spoke of his love of 'the Bohemian life' he found in 1911, when he persuaded his editor at the Winnipeg *Telegram* to establish a permanent place there, now that one of the owners of the paper had been elected to the House and was likely to be given a cabinet post. Grattan O'Leary claimed that appointment 'to the Parliamentary Press Gallery was, of course, a tremendous honour, like an appointment to the Senate.' But in fact that institution was thoroughly corrupt. When Bruce Hutchison (b. 1901) went to the Gallery for the Victoria *Times* in 1925, he 'declined the funds freely distributed by the lobbyists of business. My attitude was considered unfair and uppity, if not subversive. . . .'

Such small assaults on the status quo were not new, though they tended to take many forms. Charles A. Bowman had not been long at the Ottawa *Citizen* in 1914 when he chanced to write something about public spending that was unflattering to the Borden government. The *Citizen*'s Press Gallery correspondent passed on the message that any repetition of such behaviour 'would cause the *Citizen* to be stricken off the government's patronage list', in Bowman's words. But

> Wilson and Harry Southam [the proprietors] asked Charlie Bishop [the Gallery correspondent in question] to let the patronage minister know that the *Citizen* could get along quite happily without government patronage. Thus, after about fifty years as a Conservative party organ, my first contribution as a member of the editorial staff precipitated the *Citizen*'s declaration of political independence.

But Bowman was exaggerating the *Citizen*'s independence. O'Leary, of the rival *Journal*, admitted years later: 'At this time there were few independent newspapers in the country, most of the papers being either owned or directed by political parties or politicians, or controlled by purchasers or editors who took their politics seriously.' Ironically, it was concern about the integrity of foreign news that brought about improvement in Ottawa.

Early in the century a few papers, such as the Toronto *Telegram* and the Montreal *Star*, maintained private wires to London. The others were obliged to get their British and foreign news from the Associated Press in the United States, via the telegraphic facilities of the major Canadian railways, which had telegraphers with their brass keys stationed in the newspaper offices, sending and receiving (mostly at night). Canadian proprietors and editors were accustomed to complaining about the system, and their dissatisfaction assumed massive proportions in 1905 when the Balfour government went down to defeat in an election that saw the concurrent rise of Asquith, Lloyd George, and the young Winston Churchill. The AP had downplayed the news as being of little significance to Americans. As a result, publishers from the Lakehead to the Pacific coast met in 1907 to found a co-operative called the Western Associated Press, to which the Canadian Pacific gladly gave over its AP franchise in 1910. Similarly, and also in 1910, a co-op called the Eastern Press Association was begun in the Maritimes but was soon transformed into Canadian Press Limited, a national holding company for AP rights, and began to serve most dailies across the country, with separate services for AMs and PMs. Finally, in 1917, Canadian Press Limited merged with the eastern and western services to form a genuinely national organization with a $50,000 annual grant pledged by the Borden government. It became the Canadian Press, today's non-profit group, in 1923. With the formation of CP came a non-partisan Ottawa bureau with Press Gallery membership, sworn to report as objectively as possible, without party bias. Such standardization made the fluid nineteenth-century style coverage of Parliament an impossibility.

In provincial politics the old ways retained their usefulness for some years. As late as the 1930s, for example, the Victoria *Times* and the Victoria *Colonist* were being fed cash by the provincial Liberals and Tories respectively, though by then only the front pages and the editorial pages were for hire. In the federal arena, however, the intense party feelings, so much a part of the nineteenth century, were beginning to cool. No doubt the lowering of such passions owed much to social upheavals and attitudinal shifts arising out of the Great War. Signs of the new age were everywhere. In 1936 the masthead of *Le Soleil* in Quebec City dropped the statement that the paper was the '*organe liberal*', a line that had appeared for sixty years. The change may have suggested that *Le Soliel* was lying low during the Duplessis years, yet it was clearly part of a longer-term transition, for in 1957 the paper abandoned official political connections altogether.

The story is often told of a headline written by Harry Hindmarsh that appeared in the Toronto *Daily Star* in 1949 during the federal election campaign. Camillien Houde, the former mayor of Montreal, was seeking a seat for the Conservative party, then headed by George Drew, the former Ontario premier. The front-page banner read:

KEEP CANADA BRITISH

DESTROY DREW'S HOUDE

GOD SAVE THE KING.

It has proved memorable simply because it was no longer done to be so frank. What would have been responsible enthusiasm in 1909 had become gauche and racist in 1949.

6

ORIGINS OF THE MODERN NEWSPAPER

One Canadian press historian, W.H. Kesterton, cites the year 1913 as the zenith of Canadian newspaper publishing, what with the disappearance of so many dailies during and immediately after the Great War, mostly through amalgamation. But in fact what was taking place was the rise of the modern (one might almost say modernist) newspaper, one that was free of petty politics to an extent that would have bewildered the Victorians and that was becoming a product to be marketed, if also a public resource to be conserved. A single long generation earlier, a city of two hundred thousand people might have had five or six dailies at any given time, but most such enterprises were fluid and unstable and the products themselves were usually only eight or, later, sixteen pages; it is entirely possible that the amount of reading matter from all of them did not equal what is found today in a single issue of the Toronto *Star* or the Edmonton *Journal*. Such final realignments were well underway by the 1920s, and anyone wishing to understand contemporary newspapers might wish to make a quick survey of that decade, which represents the last phase of the evolution that began in the colonial period.

As metropolitan newspapers grew in bulk, so did the necessary infrastructure become larger and more complex, a trend that was felt proportionately all the way down the roster, affecting even papers of modest size, in smaller areas, such as the *Daily Star* of Sault Ste Marie. The paper was founded in 1901, as a weekly, by James W. Curran (1865-1951), who had been at the Montreal *Herald* after being declared redundant by the merger of the *Mail* and the *Empire* in Toronto. It became a daily in 1912, and by the 1920s had grown to 24 pages, using a press (bought second-hand from the *Border Cities Star* in Windsor) that would be augmented time and again but was not actually replaced until after the Second World War. It employed essentially the same technology as the largest papers but simply used less of it, at no sacrifice to speed.

And speed was of vital importance in that era, when continuing news stories tended to be pursued as so much melodrama and urban dailies might print as may as six editions per day, replating pages as necessary. In the 1920s, and for years afterwards, the Toronto evening papers, for example, published 'Late Closing Markets' editions, which carried the day's closing share prices and were available for sale only a half-hour or so after the three o'clock bell signalled the end of trading on the city's two stock exchanges. In the temporal sense, news seemed to come in strata, but though there were popular papers and élite ones, Canada did not participate in the movement towards tabloid papers, which both the United States and Britain were embracing at this time, each in its different way. Yet some of the characteristics of the world view that the tabloids represented could not be avoided. For their news content alone, photographs grew almost as important as stories, and by the 1920s it was possible to transmit them by wire. A number of people in various countries are given credit for inventing the process, and in truth the technology does seem to have many parents, including a Canadian, the future espionage leader Sir William Stephenson (1896-1989). He made his fortune through a photo-transmission device employing the principles found in early television; it used a photo-electric cell and two synchronized scanning disks, through which a light beam would pass, detecting varying intensities of reflected light on the image to be sent. The public became familiar with the sight of photographers, armed with flash cameras such as the ubiquitous Speed Graphic. But then such was the pull of the newspapers' own internal folklore, as shown in novels, the cinema, and other popular arts, that ordinary citizens formed lasting impressions of how newspapers worked. They would share the excitement as the news vendor cried out the reason for an 'Extra' and think themselves quite savvy and sophisticated in knowing, for instance, to ask for the city editor when phoning in a tip on a local story.

By the 1920s, then, the press had become less of an institution, perhaps, but individual papers, the ones that survived the rationalization, behaved in a more institutional manner. The freedom to do so was their reward for cunning persistence and, in many cases, was a virtual guarantee of prosperity. Accordingly they thought of themselves as necessary and powerful components of the social clockwork, and they looked the part, too. By 1928 the Toronto *Daily Star* could print an 80-page paper in the 23-storey Gothic skyscraper it was erecting, which would make a famous address of 80 King Street West, and the Calgary *Herald* was bragging of its 'ten-storey, marble, stone and terra cotta, steel fabric, fire-proof building, one of the handsomest and best equipped newspaper structures in the world, topped with a broadcasting station.'

This last detail was particularly arresting. During the Winnipeg General Strike of May-June 1919, the *Western Labour Press* published a 'General Strike Edition' extra and the *Free Press* an anti-strike edition. The Canadian Pacific telegraphers were among those taking part in the protest, and their colleagues in Edmonton and Calgary went so far as to refuse to transmit copy that originated in Winnipeg (prefiguring the national telegraphers' strike of 1924). So with the city somewhat cut off from the rest of the country, the *Free Press* installed a radio transmitter atop what would one day be called 'the Old Lady of Carlton Street' to send news to the outside world. In the next ten years, many of the pioneering commercial radio stations were in fact begun by the more enterprising daily newspapers, such as CJGC (later CFPL) of the London *Free Press* and CFCA of the Toronto *Daily Star*. But such responses, and the deliberate avoidance of such responses by others, were little more than anxious reactions to the threat that radio posed. In 1924, 6,500 Winnipegers crowded outside the *Free Press* to hear a blow-by-blow description of the championship fight between Jack Dempsey and Luis Firpo, but many more got the same news without venturing abroad. Although newsreels, too, presented a fresh challenge to the press, they were not the object of the same type of concern for the simple reason that they were not an advertising medium as well. Many newspaper proprietors grew almost irrational in their fear of radio. The Montreal *Star*, for example, remained an editorial innovator throughout this period, displaying great and lordly initiative in every facet of the paper, from running civic-improvement campaigns to maintaining more foreign bureaus than other Canadian papers, but it practically refused to acknowledge that radio existed. The policy was redoubled in the 1930s once the Canadian Broadcasting Corporation was created. In Toronto the *Globe and Mail* continued to behave in this way well into the 1950s when, in most publishers' hearts, dread of radio had long since been replaced by dread of television.

By the 1920s, writing style alone was enough to distinguish popular papers from élite ones, but publications in both camps were more alike than they were dissimilar, though columns and other such materials added a note of distinction. Some columns were quite literate and well considered, such as those of J.V. McAree (1876-1958) in the *Mail and Empire* and later in the *Globe and Mail* or those of Thomas B. Robertson (d. 1935) and others in the *Manitoba Free Press*, which continued, until comparatively recently, under the editorship of Tom Kent (b. 1922), to aspire to the level of the Fleet Street broadsheets. The Fleet Street diary column, consisting of a variety of items produced by a team using a single collective name, never caught on in the Canadian press, but pseudonyms were still common, though they tended to mirror the writer's personality as much as mask it, and invariably went to the grave along with the columnist. From 1923 until his death, E.W. Harrold (1889-1945) wrote 'The Diary of Our Own Samuel Pepys' in the Ottawa *Citizen*, using the parody form to comment on local events; and from 1943 to 1953 the novelist Robertson Davies (b. 1913) wrote a witty commentary on the Canadian scene, 'The Diary of Samuel Marchbanks', for the Peterborough *Examiner*. In other cases, columnists pursued celebrity through a cult of personality, in the American manner, and where one such figure met with success, the rival newspaper would be forced to compete, in this as in all other areas. James

Butterfield (1879-1941) of the Vancouver *Province*, for example, carried on such a column-writing contest with Bob Bouchette (d. 1936) of the *Sun*.

Looked at now, newspapers of that era seem to have been places where rigid modernity coexisted happily with a joyful archaism. The dominant labour body was the International Typographical Union, which permitted printers with paid-up union cards to wander at will from one chapel, or local, to another. Such 'travelling brothers' might work only a few months on one paper before moving on to some other part of the country, at their own libertarian pace. A few such people, who were also known as 'typos' or just plain 'tramp printers', could be found even after the Second World War. It was also during the 1920s, however, that a university education became, if not a requirement for reporters starting out in the business, at least ceased being a freaky anomaly; and more and more people could be found in newsrooms who had got their first taste of ink at student publications such as the *Ubyssey*, the *Varsity*, and the *McGill Daily*. Wages were not always commensurate with such education, however, and certainly the work itself was onerous and the hours long. Many memoirs attest innocently to conditions at that time. A reporter might begin work early in the morning, interviewing disembarking rail or steamboat passengers, rewrite stories from the rival papers or use his imagination to flesh out one arriving in abbreviated form on the 'pony wire', before proceeding to his regular beats, such as the hotels, the police station, or the lower courts (many reporters acquired as much legal knowledge as any *nisi prius* lawyer). The mid-day meal was likely to be a free one, given in exchange for covering a speech at a service club, while the evening might be taken up with a political rally or burlesque performance or whatever other event might be taking place that demanded no admission fee, at least of sympathetic reporters. For such 16-hour days, a person in the 1920s might expect to earn $20 to $25 per week, a level unchanged since the labour shortage caused by the Great War.

By 1920 newspaper proprietors had organized themselves under the banner of the Canadian Daily Newspaper Publishers' Association, but they were naturally loath to permit reporters a mutual-aid organization of their own. An attempt at a Montreal press club a few years later had to confront the publishers' fears that such gathering places were an invitation not to alcoholism but to unionism; the present Montreal Press Club was not established until 1948. This date coincided roughly with the spread of what was then called the American Newspaper Guild, though the first attempts to import this then rather militant union had taken place in Vancouver more than a decade earlier and were unsuccessful. In time the ANG supplanted the ITU as the principal union of the industry, but not before a strike in Winnipeg in 1945 resulted at one point in a crudely produced combined edition of the *Free Press* and the *Tribune*, a practice followed in other cities as the strike spread across the country and became particularly bloody in Vancouver. The three Toronto papers locked out the ITU in 1964 in a dispute that lingered, weakly, until 1971. Ironically the urge towards collective action in the editorial sector grew only after technology was cutting off the reporters and editors from the working-class, craft-based aspect of newspapers. Now, because of electronics, the old blue-collar part of newspaper production has largely disappeared, except insofar as actual press-work is concerned. When, in the 1940s, George V. Ferguson, a former Dafoeite who had become the editor of the Montreal *Star*, began to popularize the word 'craft' in reference to newspaper reporting, it was an instance of the hunter taking the name of the beast he had killed.

It was also in the 1920s that the metropolitan newspaper first came to be perceived routinely in the terms of a franchise, as a kind of privately owned utility, free of any government control or regulation and enormously lucrative if managed correctly. For that reason, business people became even more eager to own papers, just as politicians once had been; and the scheming and planning could go on for years. When Lord Atholstan died in 1938 (offending the staff of the Montreal *Star* by leaving them only one dollar each per year of service), the paper passed to the sugar baron and financier John Wilson McConnell under the terms of a deal that had been in the works for twenty years or more. A New

Brunswick businessman, H.R. Robinson, who already had a hand in a great variety of ventures, spent much of the 1920s acquiring all four dailies in Saint John and rendering them into only two, the *Times-Globe* and the *Telegraph-Journal*, which later became the pillars of K.C. Irving's media empire in that province. In a similar vein, it was to ensure a bigger slice of the pie for themselves that some proprietors began buying out long-established rivals, as when Atholstan took over the Montreal *Herald*, then killed it, and William Southam (1854-1932) of the Hamilton *Spectator* did the same with regard to the Hamilton *Times*, keeping it alive for only as long as was necessary for the *Spectator* to consolidate its hold on the local market. Even new papers could be begun, or old ones revamped, in the certainty that they would attract purchase offers. Such was the case in 1922 when entrepreneurs began a paper in Windsor and one month later sold it to the *Border Cities Star* (which became the *Windsor Star* in 1939). The right of monopoly, or near-monopoly, was often a paper's most important asset.

Competition was shrinking, but this only caused some publishers to make last-minute bids for market-share or territorial expansion. In Toronto Joseph E. Atkinson of the *Daily Star* spent several years of the 1920s and at least $250,000 in an unsuccessful attempt to make the London *Advertiser* a tenable competitor of the London *Free Press*. But the hour was late and it was already clear which papers were destined to be the dominant ones, even though decades might pass before the final hand was played. For example, circulation in the PM market in Toronto was dominated by the *Evening Telegram* throughout the 1920s—indeed in the whole period from the 1890s until the Second World War. In advertising, however, the *Telegram* was steadily losing to the *Star*. '*Telegram* business policies, before and after the death of its founder [John Ross Robertson, in 1918], remain an unsolved riddle of the Canadian newspaper world', M.E. Nichols wrote in the 1940s. 'A variety of theories has been offered; most of them overlook or underrate the possibility (by no means remote) that indications of business negligence on the part of the *Telegram* were actually the manifestation of most unusual but fully considered policy.' Robertson

> appeared to be resentful of business growth that called for expenditure on plant and buildings. A fat bank account meant much to his mental comfort, and he always had one. The fast-growing circulation of the *Telegram* at the turn of the century was to him more disturbing than gratifying. It meant that he would be driven to the expense of buying new presses.

Two later proprietors, George McCullagh and John Bassett, never regained the advantage, and the paper was closed in 1971.

One of the most far-reaching features of the 1920s was the rise of newspaper chains. The Hamilton *Spectator* had come to William Southam back in 1877, when it seemed on the verge of collapse because the Conservatives, who supported it financially, had fallen from grace and power. Southam made it a success, and then, with his sons, had obtained control of the Ottawa *Citizen* (1897), the Calgary *Herald* (1908), and the Edmonton *Journal* (1912). The *Tribune* of Winnipeg followed in 1920 and the *Province* of Vancouver in 1923. As business people, the Southams always stayed true to their roots in the printing trades. As publishers they were loyal to the Conservatives on their editorial pages, but would no more orchestrate the news columns to help the party than they would promote Christian Science (another Southam affiliation). The Siftons, who created the other newspaper chain of the period, were different, moving from the Winnipeg *Free Press* to the Regina *Leader-Post* and the Saskatoon *Star-Phoenix*, but splitting in the third generation, with one grandson, Victor (1897-1961), keeping the Winnipeg paper and his brother Clifford (1873-1976) the Saskatchewan ones. Both Siftons later threw in their lot with a small band of other publishers to found the FP Publications group, which would also include the *Globe and Mail* and a half-interest, with Southam, in Pacific Press Ltd. The latter was the joint venture that produced both the *Sun* and the *Province* in Vancouver, an accord that was designed to permit them some measure of competition, which the columnist Scott Young likened to 'a wrestling match between Siamese twins'. FP was in turn subsumed into the Thomson group. Six months later, in September 1980, Thomson prompted a federal Royal commission on newspapers (the second one in a generation) when it killed off the Ottawa *Journal* the same day that Southam put the Winnipeg *Tribune* to the sword.

Architectural historians have analysed how old buildings, if they are to endure, must survive a hazardous but relatively short period during which they have become obsolete but have not yet entered the public's perceptions about its own heritage: when it is less expensive for the owners to raze them and pay less property tax than to let them go on standing without sufficient return. A similar theory might be worked out for newspaper ownership. Ottawa had two competing English-language broadsheets for so long because the recession of 1921 and other factors put an end to an agreement made a few years previously, by which the two would have shared the cost of building circulation as well as net advertising revenues, a treaty that even involved a stock transfer and left the city one step away from an actual merger. And who knows what might have happened to the Vancouver *Sun* if the deal described by Bruce Hutchison, in which Victor Sifton's cheque for its purchase was on its way to the West Coast, had not fallen through? Newspapers have become more desirable to own as the total number of them has shrunk and the cost of beginning one from scratch has risen beyond reasonable levels. Toronto is one of only three or four cities in North America to have seen a genuinely successful start-up in the past two generations.

A mountain of precedent relating to newspaper closures tends to suggest that newspapers go out of business when competing ones have been disproportionately lucrative, and perhaps greedy. Few casualties were reported in periods when all papers have suffered, as during the Depression. Of course that is not to deny that newspapers were generally miserable in the 1930s; layoffs and salary cuts were standard practice, and business was so difficult that the Regina *Leader-Post*, for example, resorted to accepting chickens in payment for subscriptions. But the greater danger to newspapers and their readers was the tendency towards extremism that marked politics generally. In some cases the press was a force for moderation, in other cases not. In 1938 the Pulitzer Prize selection committee in New York made an exception to the rule that only American publications are eligible and awarded a medal to the Edmonton *Journal*, then under the direction of John

M. Imrie (1883-1942); it received the honour for its spirited and successful fight against the provincial Press Act of 1937, with which Alberta's Social Credit government hoped to restrict political expression. The Supreme Court of Canada declared the Act unconstitutional, whereupon the provincial government attempted to buy the Calgary *Albertan*. Then there is the matter of George McCullagh (1905-52), who merged the *Globe* and the *Mail and Empire* in 1936 to make the *Globe and Mail* and later acquired the Toronto *Telegram* as well; he founded a political movement called the Leadership League that was at best anti-democratic and perhaps even fascistic in its sympathies.

Beginning in the 1920s, and extending into the early 1930s, such devices as the Ludlow typecaster and the Elrod stripcaster, which produced headings and borders respectively, and the tape-fed teleprinter, which replaced the brass telegraph key, became increasingly common; but except for the fact that presses continued to grow faster and bigger, the pace of technological change was comparatively slow until photo-composition, and then computer typesetting, came into play in the 1970s. Editorial methods changed more quickly for a time. Such events as the 1939 Royal Tour showed how resources could be marshalled for saturation coverage, but after the Second World War a few papers began to cultivate an air of grey understatement, as though to distance themselves from the fractious rabble. William Weintraub was recalling such a period on the Montreal *Gazette* in his 1961 novel *Why Rock the Boat*, which concerns a fictitious paper named the *Daily Witness*.

> The other Montreal papers occasionally ran stories that were quite absorbing, but the Witness was beyond that. And Witnessmen were proud of the massive boredom their paper was able to achieve; there was a certain grandeur about it that only professionals could fully appreciate.

In quite another connection the large newspapers began to think in terms of Saturday packages, with fulsome amusements sections and magazines such as *Weekend*, founded in 1942. These, to our eyes, contrast sharply with those facets of a newspaper that seemed charming reminiscences of an earlier age, reminders that did not need to be large to be evocative. One appears to be looking back on a quite distant past, for example, when, in *The Style Book of the [Toronto] Evening Telegram* from 1947, one learns that military etiquette sometimes demands the use of '*OS* which is [the] abbreviation for officer's servant.'

There were some major losses in the postwar period, such as the Winnipeg *Citizen*, a co-operative paper that stopped in 1949, and the Edmonton *Bulletin*, which ceased publication in 1951. But the era seems most remarkable now as the last in which great individual proprietors, people such as Donald Cromie of the Vancouver *Sun*, Max Bell of the Calgary *Albertan*, and Victor Sifton of the Winnipeg *Free Press*, imposed their will and their personalities on the newspaper landscape before corporatism became almost universal in the industry and when a small number of superior editors, such as Oakley Dalgleish of the *Globe and Mail*, raised standards all round. Yet there is this to be said of such corporatism: it did finally bring an end to the party press. As early as 1963 the Toronto *Telegram* endorsed the Liberals in the federal election campaign, while the Vancouver *Sun* came out for the Conservatives in 1972. The world turned upside down indeed. Through it all, somehow, Canadian newspapers retained the role they achieved very early in their history. As engines of democracy and culture, they are almost laughably imperfect most of the time, but engines of a sort they continue to be.

SELECTED BIBLIOGRAPHY

BARBOUR, NOEL ROBERT. *Those Amazing People! The Story of the Canadian Magazine Industry 1778-1967*. Toronto: Crucible Press, 1982.

BILKEY, PAUL. *Persons, Papers and Things*. Toronto: Ryerson, 1940. The author, who became the editor of the Montreal *Gazette*, entered journalism in Toronto in 1896.

BOWMAN, CHARLES A. *Ottawa Editor*. Sidney, B.C.: Gray's Publishing, 1966. Re the Ottawa *Citizen* 1914-45.

BRAULT, LUCIEN et al., eds. *A Century of Reporting: The National Press Club Anthology/Un siècle de reportage: anthologie du Cercle National des Journalistes*. Toronto: Clarke, Irwin, 1967.

BRUCE, CHARLES. *News and the Southams*. Toronto: Macmillan of Canada, 1968. Commissioned corporate history.

BUSH, EDWARD F. '*The Dawson Daily News*: Journalism in the Klondike', *Canadian Historic Sites: Occasional Papers in Archaeology and History* 21, 1979.

CARELESS, J.M.S. *Brown of The Globe*. 2 vols. Toronto: Macmillan of Canada, 1959, 1963.

CARROLL, JOCK. *The Death of the Toronto Telegram & Other Newspaper Stories*. Richmond Hill, Ont.: Pocket Books, 1971.

__________. *The Life & Times of Greg Clark, Canada's Favourite Storyteller*. Toronto: Doubleday Canada, 1981.

CARTER, ALIXE. *Stop the Press—I've Made a Little Error: Notes on a Career 1932-82*. Ottawa: Sunnybrae Books, 1984. Memoirs of an Ottawa *Journal* reporter who started on the Calgary *Herald* in the 1930s.

CASH, GWEN. *Off the Record: The Personal Reminiscences of Canada's First Woman Reporter*. Langley: Stagecoach Publishing, 1977.

CHALMERS, FLOYD S. *Both Sides of the Street: One Man's Life in Business and the Arts in Canada*. Toronto: Macmillan of Canada, 1983. The author entered journalism as a reporter on the Toronto *News* and became a magazine executive.

__________. *A Gentleman of the Press*. Toronto: Doubleday Canada, 1969.

Authorized biography of the magazine publisher Col. John B. Maclean.

CHARLESWORTH, HECTOR. *Candid Chronicles: Leaves from the Note Book of a Canadian Journalist.* Toronto: Macmillan of Canada, 1925.

COLQUHOUN, A.H.U. *The Life and Letters of Sir John Willison, Journalist and Correspondent of the Times.* Toronto: Macmillan of Canada, 1935.

COMPARATOR, FRANK E. *Chronicles of Genius and Folly: R. Hoe & Company and the Printing Press as a Service to Democracy.* Culver City, California: Labyrinthos, 1979.

COOK, RAMSAY. *The Politics of John W. Dafoe and the Free Press.* Toronto: University of Toronto Press, 1963.

CRANSTON, J. HERBERT. *Ink on My Fingers.* Toronto: Ryerson Press, 1953. The author was the editor of the Toronto *Star Weekly.*

DEARMOND, R.N. *'Stroller' White: Tales of Klondike Newsman.* Vancouver: Mitchell Press, 1969.

DEMPSEY, LOTTA. *No Life for a Lady.* Toronto: Musson, 1976. The author was a reporter in Edmonton from 1923 and later in Toronto.

DEMPSON, PETER. *Assignment Ottawa: Seventeen Years in the Press Gallery.* Toronto: General Publishing, 1968.

DOYLE, RICHARD J. *Hurly-Burly: A Time at the Globe.* Toronto: Macmillan of Canada, 1989. The author was editor of the *Globe and Mail,* 1963-83.

EGGLESTON, WILFRID. *The Frontier and Canadian Letters.* Toronto: Ryerson Press, 1957.

__________. *While I Still Remember, A Personal Record.* Toronto: Ryerson Press, 1968. The author joined the Toronto *Star* in 1926, then was a university journalism instructor from 1947.

FAIRLEY, MARGARET, ed. *The Selected Writings of William Lyon Mackenzie.* Toronto: Oxford University Press, 1960.

FAUTEAU, AEGIDIUS. *The Introduction of Printing into Canada, A Brief History.* Montreal: Rolland Paper Company, 1930.

FELTEAU, CYRILLE. *Histoire de La Presse.* 2 vols. Montreal: *La Presse,* 1983-4. Commissioned corporate history.

FERGUSON, TED. *Kit Coleman: Queen of Hearts.* Toronto: Doubleday Canada, 1978. A collection of Coleman's writings, arranged thematically and with linking commentary by the editor.

FILION, GERARD. *En guise de mémoires*. Montreal: Editions du Boréal, 1989. The author was the editor of *Le Devoir*, 1947-63.

FIRTH, EDITH G. *Early Toronto Newspapers 1793-1867. A catalogue of newspapers published in the Town of York and the City of Toronto from the beginning to Confederation.* Toronto: Toronto Public Library, 1961.

FORD, ARTHUR R. *As the World Wags On.* Toronto: Ryerson Press, 1950. The author joined the Winnipeg *Telegram* in 1905 and was an editorial executive at the London *Free Press* from 1920.

FULFORD, ROBERT. *Best Seat in the House: Memoirs of a Lucky Man.* Toronto: Collins, 1988. The author was associated with the *Globe and Mail* from 1949 and the Toronto *Star* from 1958, and was the editor of *Saturday Night*, 1968-87.

GELLER, J.D. *It's Jake With Me*. Markham, Ont.: PaperJacks, 1983. Memoir by a wholesale news agent and circulation consultant, 1918-70.

GOLDENBERG, SUSAN. *The Thomson Empire*. Toronto: Methuen, 1984.

GREENWAY, ROY. *The News Game*. Toronto: Clarke, Irwin, 1966. The author was a Toronto *Star* reporter, 1918-61.

GRIFFIN, FREDERICK. *Variety Show: Twenty Years of Watching the News Parade*. Toronto: Macmillan of Canada, 1936. The author joined the Toronto *Star* in 1916 and became perhaps Canada's most accomplished general reporter.

HAIG, KENNETHE M. *Brave Harvest: The Life Story of E. Cora Hind, LL.D.* Toronto: Thomas Allen, 1945.

HANN, RUSSELL.'Brainworkers and the Knights of Labor: E.E. Sheppard, Phillips Thompson, and the *Toronto News*, 1883-1887', in *Essays in the Canadian Working Class History*, edited by Gregory S. Kealey and Peter Warrian. Toronto: McClelland & Stewart, 1976.

HARKNESS, ROSS. *J.E. Atkinson of the Star*. Toronto: University of Toronto Press, 1963. Commissioned corporate history.

HENDRY, PETER. *Epitaph for Nostalgia: A Personal Memoir of the Death of The Family Herald by Its Last Editor*. Montreal: Agri-World Press, 1968.

'How Can Canadian Universities Best Benefit the Profession of Journalism, as a Means of Moulding and Elevating Public Opinion?'. A

Collection of Essays. Toronto: Copp Clark, 1903.

HUTCHISON, BRUCE. *The Far Side of the Street*. Toronto: Macmillan of Canada, 1976. The author was the editor of the Victoria *Daily Times*, where he began his career in 1918, and of the Vancouver *Sun*.

JOHNSON, J. GEORGE. *The Weeklies: Biggest Circulation in Town*. Bolton, Ont.: Canadian Weekly Newspapers Association, 1972.

KEATE, STUART. *Paper Boy*. Toronto: Clarke, Irwin, 1980. The author was associated with the Vancouver *Province* and the Vancouver *Sun*, 1935-78.

KESTERTSON, W.H. *A History of Journalism in Canada*. Toronto: McClelland & Stewart, 1967. A survey.

KING, ANDREW. *Pen, Paper & Printing Ink*. Saskatoon: Western Producer Prairie Books, 1970. King was the proprietor of various Prairie weeklies from 1905.

LAMB, JAMES B. *Press Gang: Post-war Life in the World of Canadian Newspapers*. Toronto: Macmillan of Canada, 1979. The author describes the emasculation of the Orillia *Daily Packet and Times* by the Thomson chain.

LEGATE, DAVID M. *Fair Dinkum*. Toronto: Doubleday Canada, 1969. The memoirs of a Montreal *Star* reporter.

LIVESAY, J.F.B. *The Making of a Canadian*, edited and with a memoir by Florence Randal Livesay. Toronto: Ryerson, 1947. The author became a journalist in Winnipeg in 1903 and was associated with the Canadian Press until 1939.

LYNCH, CHARLES. *You Can't Print That!* Edmonton: Hurtig Publishers, 1983. Memoirs of an Ottawa columnist who worked on Saint John and Halifax papers in the 1930s and for CP.

MacEWAN, GRANT. *Eye Opener Bob, The Story of Bob Edwards*. Saskatoon: Western Producer Book Service, 1974.

MacFARLANE, ANDREW. *It Seemed Like a Good Idea at the Time*. Toronto: Nonpareil Canada, 1983. A running memoir of the Toronto *Telegram* used as a thread to connect some of the author's columns therefrom.

MacGILLIVRAY, GEORGE B. *A History of Fort William and Port Arthur Newspapers from 1875*. Toronto: Bryant Press, 1968.

McNAUGHT, CARLTON. *Canada Gets the News*. Toronto: Ryerson Press, 1940. Analysis of foreign news in Canadian newspapers.

MILLER, ORLO. *A Century of Western Ontario: The Story of London, 'The Free Press', and Western Ontario, 1849-1949*. Toronto: Ryerson, 1949. Commissioned corporate history.

Montreal Gazette: A Tradition Lives. The Story of the Montreal Gazette. Montreal: The Gazette, 1954? Commissioned corporate history.

MUNRO, RAYMOND Z. *The Sky's the Limit.* Toronto: Key Porter, 1985. Memoir by a photographer-reporter and thus unusual; Toronto *Star* of 1940s-50s.

NICHOLS, M.E. *(CP) The Story of the Canadian Press.* Toronto: Ryerson Press, 1948.

NOLAN, MICHAEL. *Walter J. Blackburn: A Man for All Media.* Toronto: Macmillan of Canada, 1989. Commissioned biography of the proprietor of the London *Free Press.*

O'LEARY, GRATTAN. *Recollections of People, Press, and Politics.* Toronto: Macmillan of Canada, 1977. Re the Ottawa *Journal*, 1911-66.

POULTON, RON. *Life in a Word Factory.* Toronto: Toronto Sun Publishing, 1976. Commissioned corporate history.

__________. *The Paper Tyrant: John Ross Robertson of the Toronto Telegram.* Toronto: Clarke, Irwin, 1971. Commissioned corporate history.

RABOY, MARC. *Movements and Messages: Media and Radical Politics in Quebec*, translated by David Homel. Toronto: Between the Lines, 1984.

ROBERTS, WAYNE. 'The Last Artisans: Toronto Printers, 1896-1914', in *Essays in Canadian Working Class History*, edited by Gregory S. Kealey and Peter Warrian. Toronto: McClelland & Stewart, 1976.

ROSS, PHILIP DANSKEN. *Retrospects of a Newspaper Person.* Toronto: Oxford University Press, 1931. The author was the editor of the Ottawa *Journal.*

ROWLAND, BARRY D., and J. DOUGLAS MacFARLANE. *The Maple Leaf Forever: The Story of Canada's Foremost Armed Forces Newspaper.* Toronto: Natural Heritage, 1987.

RUTHERFORD, PAUL. *The Making of the Canadian Media.* Toronto: McGraw-Hill Ryerson, 1978. A survey.

__________. *A Victorian Authority: The Daily Press in Late Nineteenth-Century Canada.* Toronto: University of Toronto Press, 1982. The single most thoughtful and informative source.

SCHRADER, E.U. and E.R. JOHNSTON. *Campus Reporter: A Cub Reporter's Introduction to Newspaper Work.* Ottawa: Canadian University Press, 1963.

SEARS, VAL. *Hello Sweetheart . . . Get Me Rewrite.* Toronto: Key Porter Books, 1988. Re the Toronto newspaper wars, 1952-71.

SIGGINS, MAGGIE. *Bassett: John Bassett's Forty Years in Politics, Publishing, Business and Sports.* Toronto: James Lorimer, 1979.

SMITH, I. NORMAN, ed. *The Diary of Our Own Pepys: E.W. Harrold's Record of Canadian Life.* Toronto: Ryerson Press, 1947.

__________. *The Journal Men.* Toronto: McClelland & Stewart, 1974. Sketches of three successive editors of the Ottawa *Journal.*

SOTIRON, MINKO, ed. *An Annotated Bibliography of Works on Daily Newspapers in Canada/Une bibliographie annotée des ouvrages portant sur les quotidiens canadiens, 1914-1983.* Montreal: the author, 1987.

STEEL, C. FRANK. *Prairie Editor: The Life and Times of Buchanan of Lethbridge.* Senator William Buchanan was a journalist 1897-1954, latterly as proprietor of the Lethbridge *Herald.*

STEWART, WALTER, ed. *Canadian Newspapers: The Inside Story.* Edmonton: Hurtig Publishers, 1980. An anthology of reminiscences and critiques.

The Story of the Press: Chapters in the North-West History Prior to 1890 Related by Old Timers. Battleford: Canadian North-West Historical Society Publications, Vol. 1, No. IV, Pt. 1, 1928.

STURSBERG, PETER, ed. *Extra! When the Papers Had the Only News.* Victoria: Provincial Archives of British Columbia, 1982. Sound Heritage Series No. 35. Oral history of Vancouver journalism.

__________. *Those Were the Days: The Days of Benny Nichols and the Lotus Eaters.* Toronto: Peter Martin, 1969. A memoir of the Victoria *Daily Times* in the 1930s.

SUTHERLAND, FRASER. *The Monthly Epic, A History of Canadian Magazines, 1789-1989.* Markham: Fitzhenry & Whiteside, 1989.

WARD, JOHN. *The Hansard Chronicles: A Celebration of the First Hundred Years of Hansard in Canada's Parliament.* Ottawa: Deneau and Greenburg, 1980. A worthwhile source re the colonial and reform press.

WILLISON, SIR JOHN. *Reminiscences Political and Personal.* Toronto: McClelland & Stewart, 1919.

WOLFE, MORRIS, ed. *A Saturday Night Scrapbook.* Toronto: New Press, 1973.

WOODCOCK, GEORGE. *Amor De Cosmos, Journalist and Reformer.* Toronto: Oxford University Press, 1975.

WORTHINGTON, PETER. *Looking for Trouble: A Journalist's Life and Then Some.* Toronto: Key Porter, 1984. Re the Toronto *Telegram* and the Toronto *Sun.*

YOUNG, SCOTT. *Gordon Sinclair: A Life—And Then Some.* Toronto: Macmillan of Canada, 1987.

ZERKER, SALLY F. *The Rise and Fall of the Toronto Typographical Union 1832-1972: A Case Study of Foreign Domination.* Toronto: University of Toronto Press, 1982.

ZWICKER, BARRY, and DICK MacDONALD, eds. *The News: Inside the Canadian Media.* Ottawa: Deneau, 1979. Articles from *Content* magazine.

INDEX